A COMPENDIUM OF SAUCY SONGS, DOTTY DITTIES, & MONOLOGUE MIRTH

by

Arthur MacTier

Have fun, and keep smiling!
Arthur MacTier

Pen Press Publishers Ltd

Copyright © Arthur MacTier 2008

All rights reserved

No part of this publication may be reproduced,
stored in a retrieval system, or transmitted
in any form or by any means, without
the prior permission in writing of the publisher,
nor be otherwise circulated in any form of binding or cover other
than that in which it is published and without a similar condition
including this condition being imposed on the subsequent purchaser.

* * *

The author has made every effort to apply for copyright permission for reproduction purposes, and accordingly thanks those who granted permissions as listed opposite (or within the book). Those who did not reply in the first instance are invited to contact the auther via the publishers, should they deem permission is required.

* * *

First published in Great Britain by
Pen Press Publishers Ltd
25 Eastern Place
Brighton
BN2 1GJ

ISBN 978-1-906206-59-8

Printed and bound in the UK

A catalogue record of this book is available from
the British Library

Cover design Jacqueline Abromeit

Contents

Preface

Saucy Songs   1

Side by side.	4
Are you lonesome tonight?	6
The Ballad of Burry and Freda	8
The story of Bridie McGrath.	15
While the train is in the station.	17
Down below.	18
Three old ladies locked in the lavatory.	20
Seven Irish ladies locked in the lavatory.	21
Away in the manger.	23
Once in Blunkett David's city.	25
While shepherds watched their flocks by night.	27
The laughing taxman.	29
Don't	31
As time goes by.	32
All things bright, and beautiful/The indolent vicar of Bray /I wish I were a caterpillar	34
All things dull and ugly/ When I went walking, with my uncle Jim	36
On the seventh day of Christmas/We are born crying/ Christmas epitaph	38

Dotty Ditties   41

The call of the wild.	43
Committees/Prayer before breakfast	45
The tale of dear old Flo'	47
I'm a maiden of forty	48

The undertaker's wedding	50
Silver wedding reminiscences/Romeo & Juliette	52
An infant prodigy	54
Sonia Snell	55
Last night, as I lay sleeping	57
Pete the piddling pup	58
Reminiscences of a senior citizens' tea dance	60
Senior citizens' blessings	62
Life spans/There are several reasons for drinking	63
Times gone by	65
God.com	67
The Lord's Prayer/Bankers' prayer	69
The Twins	71
The Ballad of William Bloat	73
Widow Malone	75
The dilemma of Deirdre Flynn	77
Johnny Sands	79
Alex and her	80
Tongue twister/A nod is as good as a wink	81
The Miser/Here's to our wives	83
Albert's reunion	85
I take it, you already know	88
There's no truth in all that, at all/Ten sticks of dynamite standing on the wall	89
The plaint of the camel	90
The new ABC's	92
Little Red Riding Hood, and the Big Bad Wolf (Adult version)	94
William the Conqueror	97
The toilet testament	98
A mother's lament	99
The Ballad of Bethnal Green/O come with me, and be my love	101
Merry Christmas, you suckers	103
Santa's lament	105
The illusionist's assistant	107
Today I'm 80	109

Acknowledgements

This book would not be complete without me extending grateful thanks to the following generous souls, who either contributed or inspired the creation of the items specifically referred to in each of the acknowledgements:

Una Nield, Royton, Oldham, Lancs – Re 'Down below' and also the ditty extolling my virtues!

Jean Matthews, Mansfield, Notts – Re 'Silver Wedding Reminiscences'.

Jean Edwards, Culcheth, Cheshire – Re 'Side by side'.

Elsie Crutchett, Ganswood, Wigan, Lancs – Re 'Reminiscences of a Senior Citizens' Tea Dance', and also the basis of 'Seamus O'Boyle's letter to Dr. Maloney'.

Carl Cahill, Brisbane, Australia – Re 'Pizza Hut' duologue.

Anne Hamlet, St.Helens, Lancs – Re 'The story of Bridie McGrath', & 'The dogs meeting'.

Peter Manning, Architect, Leamington Spa, Warwickshire - Re 'The company with over 500 employees', and the 'Nelson/Hardy' duologue.

Geoff Bevan, Landlord, Rose & Thistle, Haddenham, Bucks – Re 'The Sermon', and the 'London Bus Driver's Lament'.

Alastair MacBrayne, Wine Merchant, Kenilworth, Warwickshire – Re 'While the train is in the station'.

Peter Huckle, Ret'd Chartered Accountant, Leamington Spa, Warwickshire – Re 'Oh give me your pity'.

Rosalee Roberts, Pearcedale, Victoria, Australia – Re 'Sonia Snell'.

David Sheffield, North Baddesley, Southampton – Re 'Viagra'.

Michael O'Callaghan, Long Itchington, Warwickshire – Re 'Irish Blessing'.

Janet X, Wiltshire – Re 'She couldn't remember her rumba'.

Ashwin Kagdadia, Chartered Accountant, Leicester – Re 'Bush/Rice' duologue.

and finally, I am greatly indebted to Methuen Publishing for granting me permission to reproduce what is just one gem from their publication 'The Victoria Wood Song Book' – 2nd Ed'n. Copyright (c) Victoria Wood

I'm fine, thank you	112
Balanced viagra	114
Mary had a little lamb	116
A view of cruising	118
Life on a cruise ship	120
Shuffleboard aboard	122
Ship-shape	125
Jack Sprat for grown-ups/Old Methuselah/I sat next to the duchess at tea	126
She couldn't remember her rumba/I love a Martini/Giddy ditty	128
Greetings card verses	130
Try it the other way round/My father is a policeman	132
The boy stood on the burning deck/Simple Simon	135
A ditty not to be sniffed at!	137
Una's ode/Blessing	138

Monologue Mirth — 141

Rev. Abraham Blythe's letter	143
Inland Revenue letter	144
Letter to the Leith Police	146
Seamus O'Boyle's letter to his doctor/Kisses/Wedding Anniversary	150
Paddy's letter to his bank manager	153
Barnacle Bill with a difference	155
Whiff of fear	157
Life before computers	159
Whatever befalls us/Doctor Bell, fell down the well	160
A snake called Pete	161
Life in the new millennium	163
Company statistics	165
Company statistics – Answers to (i) & (ii)	166
Asylum	167
It's no lark, building an ark	170

Jack Jones' job specification	172
Quirks of the English language	174
Up yours	175
The sermon	177
The vicar	180
Glossary of the rhyming slang vocabulary	181
The secret of successful speaking/Prayer prior to speech/ Speeches are like babies/The ABC/XYZ of public speaking	183
I'm now my own grandfather!/Charlie Mopps	185
An Italian in Malta	187
Spike Milligan's introduction to Genesis/A baby sardine/ My name is Fred Fernackerpan	188
The cruiser's prayer	190
The 12 days of Christmas/In Brighton, she was Brenda	191
Paddy's toast/blessing	197

Bonus Duologues   199

Bush/Rice	200
Pizza Hut Lady/Customer	211
Nelson/Hardy	220

Epilogue (All good things come to an end – or do they?!)	**231**
An insight into Fart-ology!	231
Final blessing	242

Late night extras   243

The rules of cricket	244
The lager lout's prayer	245

Appendix   247

The ballad of Barry & Freda – Individual dialogues	248

Preface

Shortly after the great American (but British-born!) comedian Bob Hope died, his granddaughter was quoted as saying that her grandpa Bob had an ongoing ambition in life, which was to bring joy into every room he ever entered!

Hence if you, dear reader, are similarly motivated, then within the content of this Compendium, you will certainly find much ammunition to assist you in the attainment of that worthy objective.

Of course, the most common way of achieving such an objective is through the generation of laughter, and although the Oxford English Dictionary broadly defines laughter as 'the emission of spasmodic inarticulate sounds; movements of the facial muscles; or the shaking of sides, that are instinctive expressions of lively amusement, scorn, exultation, or reactions to physical sensations, such as tickling', I prefer the simpler definition: that laughter is the best medicine – not only due to the fact that, unlike other medicines, there are no side effects, but also, because laughter is:

(a) a pain killer;
(b) a cure for depression; and
(c) a tonic, which fuels the 'feel good' factor!

– though that doesn't *always* appear to be the case, as confirmed by the following:

Laugh, and the whole world laughs with you,
Is the old adage, I hear;
But when I was a lad, I laughed at me dad,
And he belted me, right in the ear!

But seriously, as very few folk have a *natural ability* to generate laughter (me included!), I decided many years ago to write down *or redevelop,* every ditty, song or monologue that I came across at functions, which had evoked mirth. Hence, whether you are a clubber; party-goer; socialite; M.C.; pub addict; circuit lecturer; local society member; or entertainer of any type, you will certainly find usable items within this Compendium, that will not only come across to your audiences as refreshingly new (as several are actually original with me), but many of which have also already been audience tested!

In particular are the three *duo*logues, of which two are an *absolute hoot* for a husband and wife to perform, and which you will find really *will* go down well with virtually any audience. Finally, for the very broad-minded, I have also included within the Epilogue a mini-thesis on Fart-ology, which even some of the most prim will discover has been very *tastefully* put together, so to speak!

For your further information and assistance, I have also provided introductory preambles, where appropriate, as well as afterthoughts, in order to highlight the ideal performance scenarios or other relevant background data. Furthermore, where appropriate, I have also endeavoured to give credit to the originators of any items that have inspired the amended versions, which now await you, and sincerely apologise for the absence of credits for any items that have been passed on to me without an indication of their source.

So without more ado, it's over to you! Have fun!

Saucy Songs

Although many entertainers *end* their performances with a song, I felt it appropriate to *begin* this compendium of aids to performance (whether merely at the dinner table, or formally, behind a mike) with a selection of *songs,* knowing that they will certainly evoke both smiles and laughter in good measure, and justification for which is exemplified by the following, familiar ditty:

> When Irish eyes are smiling,
> Sure it's like a morning spring,
> In the lilt of Irish laughter
> You can hear the angels sing.
> When Irish hearts are happy,
> All the world, seems bright and gay,
> And when Irish eyes are smiling,
> Sure, they steal your heart away!

But it is not *just* the Irish whose laughter and smiles brighten up the day; *it is in us all* to emulate their example, as the following familiar, anonymous ode duly suggests that we do:

The value of a smile

> A smile costs nothing but gives much.
> It enriches those who receive it, without making poorer those who give.
> It takes but a moment, but the memory of it sometimes lasts forever.
> None is so rich or mighty that he can get along without it.
> And none so poor that he cannot be made rich by it.
>
> A smile creates happiness in the home, and fosters goodwill in business;
> And is the countersign of friendship.

It brings rest to the weary, cheer to the discouraged, sunshine to the sad,
And is nature's best antidote for trouble,
Yet it cannot be bought, begged or stolen,
For it is something of no value to anyone, until it is given away.

Some people are too tired to give a smile – so give them one of yours,
As none needs a smile so much as he who has none to give!

In other words:
No matter how grouchy, you're feeling,
A nice smile is more or less healing,
It grows in a wreath
Around the front teeth,
And prevents the face from congealing!

Those, of course, are messages, which if understood by *everyone*, would make the world a better, and kinder place! So what are you waiting for? Move on, to the (saucy) songs!

Side by side

In a compendium as extensive as this, selection of the first item is quite difficult, so with Irish quaintness, I decided to *begin* with an audience-tested *ending*, in the guise of 'Side by side'!

It is best sung to the tune and rhythm of the familiar song 'I ain't got a barrel of money', and an ideal way of introducing it, is to tell your audience that what you are about to sing is meant to epitomise the lottery of marriage, when two people decide to 'tie the knot' after a very short courtship! The lyrics are as follows:

We got married on Sunday;
The party lasted till Monday!
When the guests were all gone,
We were alone – side by side.

We got ready for bed then;
I very nearly dropped dead then;
*Her teeth and her hair
*She placed on a chair – side by side!

(Now a slight change of melody)

*Then she took her dress off,
*To reveal her all;
*First an arm, then a leg
*She propped up against the wall!

(now return to the main song theme)

That left me bro-ken heart-ed,
With half my wife, I had parted,
So we slept on the chair;
There was more of her there – side by side!

(Then, like Ken Dodd, immediately end with a cheery 'Tatty bye'!)

*For further effect, **whilst singing** the second verse, use your hands to emphasise the placement of the teeth and the hair on a chair; and likewise, in the third verse, wave an arm and a leg – all of which will serve to intensify the comedy of the delivery, which always gets a laugh!

Are you lonesome tonight?

Continuing the man/woman relationship theme, this item always goes down well with mixed audiences and, like 'Side by side', also benefits from a punchy finish. Hence, one way of introducing it is to suggest to your audience that they will surely be familiar with Elvis Presley's hit song 'Are you lonesome tonight?' Then, by using entertainer's licence, continue by saying that what they won't know is that you were recently told he once sang a different version of that song over the phone to a lady friend who had ditched him, the lyrics of which go as follows:

> Are you lonesome tonight?
> Are your corsets too tight?
> Does your bra lie flat on your chest?
>
> Is your midriff held in
> By a large safety pin?
> Do you have a big hole in your vest?
>
> Do your piles give you gyp,
> Like the sores on your lip?
> Do your teeth drop down when you yawn?
>
> Is your hair like a wreath?
> Have you gaps in your teeth?
> Are your knickers all tattered and torn?
>
> Are your eyes growing dim?
> Is your form far from slim,
> And enough to give most men a fright?
>
> Then you should hope and pray
> You won't also turn grey,

Or by God you'll be lonesome tonight!

When delivering the last line, slow your delivery down a little and raise your voice slightly, as that will intensify the final impact.

The ballad of Barry and Freda

Although this is in effect *a duologue*, I felt it pertinent to include it within the Saucy Song section due to the fact that, for maximum impact, it needs to be delivered as a song; but as no compendium/anthology of saucy songs or dotty ditties could really be deemed adequate without featuring something of the flavour of that star of light entertainment, Victoria Wood, O.B.E., I could not set out the lyrics without first citing what, in a way, is a very well-deserved 'commercial'. Hence it is right to mention that over the last 30-odd years, Victoria has not only been a prolific writer of comedy, but has also won many awards for her wonderful contributions to the world of light entertainment, and although a number of her creations, including this one, are readily available to all via the Internet, she has also had several books published, all of which can be heartily recommended to anyone who is keen to look on the bright side of life!

Following that scenario, it won't come as a surprise to you to hear that I deem 'The Ballad of Barry and Freda' an absolute gem of an example of how comical the pairing of a sex-starved, lively lady with a lifeless, wimpish male, can be in real life. Although this can be delivered as **a solo** item, I must nevertheless mention that for maximum impact, it is best performed as **a duologue**, and thus any readers in sympathy with the latter will find that following on from the **combined** dialogue, I have also featured **separate** assemblage of Barry's own lines, and those of Freda likewise, within an appendix to make it easy for them to be reproduced.

To get into it then, simply remind your audience how frustrating married life can be, when one partner is all keyed up for a night of passion while the other is about as lifeless as a dodo, and then launch into the following:

Freda and Barry sat one night;
The sky was clear, the stars were bright,
The wind was soft, the moon was up;
Freda drained her cocoa cup.

She licked her lips, she felt sublime,
She switched off 'Gardeners' Question Time'.
Barry cringed in fear and in dread,
As Freda grabbed his tie and said:

Let's do it!
Let's do it;
Do it while the mood is right!
I'm feeling
Appealing;
I've really got an appetite!

I'm on fire
With desire;
I could handle half the tenors in a male voice choir;
Let's do it,
Let's do it tonight!

But he said:
I can't do it,
I can't do it.
I don't believe in too much sex!
This fashion
For passion
Turns us into nervous wrecks!

No derision,
My decision –
I'd rather watch The Muppets on the television!
I can't do it;
I can't do it tonight!

So she said:
Let's do it!
Let's do it,
Do it till our hearts go boom!
Go native,
Creative,
Living in the living room!

This folly
Is jolly,
Bend me over backwards on me hostess trolley
Let's do it,
Let's do it tonight!

But he said:
I can't do it,
I can't do it,
Me 'eavy breathing days have gone.
I'm older,
Feel colder,
It's other things that turn me on!

I'm imploring,
I'm boring,
Let me read this catalogue on vinyl flooring!
I can't do it;
I can't do it tonight!

So she said:
Let's do it!
Let's do it,
Have a crazy night of love!
I'll strip bare,
Just wear
Stilettos and an oven glove!

Don't starve a
Girl in a palaver;
Dangle from the wardrobe in your balaclava!
Let's do it,
Let's do it tonight!

But he said:
I can't do it,
I can't do it,
I know I'd only get it wrong.
Don't angle
For me to dangle,
Me arms 'ave never been that strong!

Stop pouting,
Stop shouting,
You know I pulled a muscle when I did the grouting!
I can't do it;
I can't do it tonight!

Let's do it,
Let's do it!
Share a night of wild romance!
Frenetic,
Poetic,
This could be your last big chance!

To quote Milton,
To eat Stilton,
To roll in gay abandon on the tufted Wilton!
Let's do it,
Let's do it tonight!

I can't do it,
I can't do it,

I've got other little jobs on hand.
Don't grouse
About the house,
I've got a busy evening planned!

Stop nagging,
I'm flagging,
You know as well as I do that the pipes want lagging
I can't do it,
I can't do it tonight!

Let's do it!
Let's do it
While I'm really in the mood!
Three cheers,
It's years
Since I caught you even semi-nude!

Be drastic,
Gymnastic,
Wear your baggy Y-fronts with the loose elastic!
Let's do it,
Let's do it tonight!

I can't do it,
I can't do it,
I must refuse to get undressed.
I feel silly,
It's too chilly
To go without me thermal vest!

Don't choose me,
Don't use me,
Me mother sent a note to say you must excuse me!
I can't do it,
I can't do it tonight!

Let's do it!
Let's do it,
I feel I absolutely must;
I won't exempt you,
Want to tempt you,
Want to drive you mad with lust!

No cautions,
Just contortions,
Smear an avocado on me lower portions!
Let's do it,
Let's do it tonight!

I can't do it,
I can't do it,
It's really not my cup of tea,
I'm harassed,
Embarrassed,
I wish you hadn't picked on me!

No dramas!
Gimme me pyjamas,
The only girl I'm mad about is Judith Chalmers!
I can't do it,
I can't do it tonight!

Let's do it,
Let's do it,
I really want to run amok,
Let's wiggle,
Let's jiggle,
Let's really make the rafters rock!

Be mighty,
Be flighty,

Come and melt the buttons on me flame-proof nightie
Let's do it,
Let's do it tonight!

Let's do it,
Let's do it,
I really want to rant and rave!
Let's go,
'Cos I know
Just how I want you to behave:

Not bleakly,
Not meekly,
Beat me on the bottom with a 'Woman's Weekly'!
Let's do it,
Let's do it tonight!

For further impact, endeavour to recite the Barry lines with a wimpish voice, and if you can do so with a Mancunian accent, that will also enhance the performance. Again, Freda's lines should be delivered speedily like a woman raring for passion!

The story of Bridie McGrath

Although this item of unknown origin can be delivered as a ditty, it is best performed as a saucy song, though for the tune you will need to enlist the help of someone who is familiar with Irish-flavoured music, in order to identify a melody which suits the rhythm of the lyrics. (Your local St Patrick's Day party would be the ideal source of such assistance, as well as an ideal platform for giving the song an airing!)

> Now I'll tell you a story that is sure to shock;
> It's all about a murder on the Ring's End Dock.
> The lady in question is Bridie McGrath,
> And she strangled two sailors with the straps of her bra!
>
> Chorus:
> With a too-ry-ah; fol-dee-diddle-ah;
> Too-ry; ooh-ry; ooh-ry-ah
>
> They tried to dope her with a foreign liqueur.
> Clever as they were, they could not trick her.
> She remembered the story told by her ma –
> Always keep your hands on the straps of your bra!
>
> Chorus:
>
> She caught the big fella by the head,
> And she flung him in the Liffey like a crust of bread.
> The other fella laughed with a ha-ha-ha,
> And she stuffed his gob with the rest of her bra!
>
> Chorus:
>
> Young ladies, when courting a sailor by night,
> Never wear the straps of your bra too tight.

Remember the story of Bridie McGrath;
Always keep your hands on the straps of your bra!

Chorus:

This ditty is typically Irish in flavour, and several more can be found within this Compendium.

While the train is in the station

Because nothing involving humans escapes the attention of the humorist, not even the needs of the toilet, the following item, when sung to the tune 'Humoresque' by Dvorak, will always go down well. A good way of getting 'into it' is by using entertainer's licence and saying that in the grand old days of steam trains, polite loudspeaker announcements would keep passengers au fait with station procedures, such as the following:

> While the train is in the station,
> Please refrain from urination.
> Have regard for railway property.
>
> If you want to pass some water,
> Go and see the railway porter,
> Who will guide you to the lavatory!
>
> Should discharge be quite a strain
> And duly make you miss your train,
> You should drink a soothing cup of tea.
>
> As when you do vacate the loo,
> Your train will be halfway to Crewe,
> The moral of all that just has to be:
>
> Give your system lubrication
> Well before you reach the station,
> And avoid a further tragedy!

Down below

For a more earthy example of toilet-flavoured items (in more ways than one!), the following is best sung rhythmically to the tune of: 'She'll be coming round the mountain when she comes':

When you're working in the sewer
Down below,
And you're feeling quite secure
Down below;
Though you're treading in manure,
And have rat bites to endure,
There is still, a strange allure
Down below.

Though at times it can be hell
Down below,
And if you accidentally fell
Down below;
Then the ruddy awful smell
Would soon make you far from well
And no longer wish to dwell
Down below.

But though you're racked with pain
Down below,
And you're missing lovely Jane
Down below.;
You'll decide you should remain
As the calling of the drain
Will have surfaced once again
Down below.

Now the moral of this tale
Down below,
Is that marriages will fail
Down below;
If the wife does not prevail
And make her man curtail
His ludicrous travail
Down below!

Three old ladies locked in the lavatory

As ever in the world of humour, tastes vary and thus one needs to be quite selective from to time to time in terms of the material one uses. So, providing you sense that your audience is reasonably broad-minded, then this offering is an ideal lead into the Irish version which follows it, and is best sung to the nursery rhyme tune of 'Oh dear, what can the matter be, Johnny's so long at the fair?'

> Oh dear, what can the matter be?
> Three old ladies locked in the lavatory;
> They were there from Monday to Saturday,
> And nobody knew they were there.
>
> The first one's name was Elizabeth Porter,
> Who went in to be rid of some water,
> But stayed in there for more than she ought to,
> And nobody knew she was there!
>
> The second one's name was Elizabeth Humphrey,
> She went in and made herself comfy,
> Then said to the girls: 'I can't get my bum free',
> But nobody knew they were there!
>
> The last one's name was Elizabeth Carter,
> She was known as a world renowned farter,
> When she was in it was like a sonata,
> But nobody knew they were there!

Seven Irish ladies locked in the lavatory

When sung to the same tune and rhythm as the preceding item, this version always goes down well with broad-minded audiences, especially if performed with an Irish accent. The lyrics are as follows:

Oh dear what can the matter be?
Seven Irish ladies locked in the lavatory;
They were there from Monday to Saturday,
And nobody knew they were there!

Being on their way for a chat with the vicar,
They went in together 'cos they thought it'd be quicker,
But they couldn't get out, as the door was a sticker,
And nobody knew they were there!

The first old lady was soon in a spot
As she hadn't a coin to put in the slot,
And to hold it all back, she got in a knot,
But nobody knew they were there!

The next old lady, whose name was just Nell,
Did quickly pass out because of the smell!
In a few short minutes the place was like Hell,
And nobody knew they were there!

One of the ladies was Deidre Mason,
Who no longer could wait, so used the big basin,
Not knowing the Pope once washed his good face in,
And nobody knew they were there!

The next old lady was Hilary Fender,
Who was doing alright until her suspender
Got all tangled up in her feminine gender!
But nobody knew they were there!

The next old lady was Bridie O'Toole,
And after performing she felt like a fool,
As her toilet was blocked and she left quite a pool,
But nobody knew they were there!

The next old lady was Elizabeth Hart,
Who sat for ten minutes, trying to start,
But all she could do was to sit there and fart,
And nobody knew they were there!

The last of the seven, was Sophia Draper,
But when she sat down, she found there's no paper,
So she rolled up a towel to use as a scraper,
And nobody knew they were there!

As the experience had been very scary,
They prayed for release with a Hail Mary,
The door did then open as if by a fairy,
And now nobody need know they were there!

Away in a manger

Although the public's memory of news items that were quite significant at the time of their occurrence tends to be short **at best**, it is nevertheless easy enough to revive such memories through the medium of humour, especially where the personalities involved were very well known at the time. A prime example of this was the considerable press coverage of the affair involving South Derbyshire M.P. Edwina Currie, and the then Prime Minister, John Major, which emerged following the publication of Edwina's book Currie's Diaries 2002. Not surprisingly, the affair prompted a creative Daily Express columnist, with the pseudonym 'Beachcomber', to capitalise on the humorous aspect by substituting the lyrics of the popular Christmas Carol 'Away in the manger', as follows:

Away in Westminster,
In a large double bed,
A Derbyshire member
Laid down her sweet head,

And lying beside her
In illicit embrace
Was a man dressed in grey,
With a smile on his face!

Edwina and Johnny;
Who'd have thought it of them?
She'd had it away
With the nation's P.M.!

Away with John Major,
It can't be denied
That this greyest of men
Had a bit on the side!

A government warning:
Though ingested with stealth,
A night on the Currie
Can damage your health!

Before performing this item, it is in your interests to preface it with a short introduction, in which you:

(a) rhetorically ask your audience whether they had a nice Christmas. Daft as it seems, you should make that enquiry during **any month** from January to October **inclusive**, as the later in the year it is, the question's unusual nature will generate keen audience focus, and even a chuckle! For November and December, simply ask them if they are looking forward to Christmas and, irrespective of any response, duly proceed to state that to get them in the mood, you will now sing a familiar carol.

(b) Always remember to mention that Edwina Currie was M.P. for South Derbyshire, which duly confirms the relevance of that county featured in the first verse.

Once in Blunkett David's city

In similar vogue, but perhaps not quite so widely publicised, was a trio of alleged misdemeanours that involved Labour M.P. for Sheffield Brightside, David Blunkett, featuring an affair with a married woman; the fathering of a baby; plus alleged irregularities regarding the provision of visas for a nanny. Quite a guy, bearing in mind his blindness since birth! Again, 'Beachcomber' of the Daily Express saw the humorous side of it all, and duly came up with a droll version thereof, in the guise of another popular Christmas carol, 'Once in Royal David's City':

> Once in Blunkett David's city
> Stood a lonely maiden wed.
> Now a mother with a baby,
> After David took this maid to bed!
> He proclaimed in voice quite wild:
> 'I'm the father of your child!'
>
> He came down in chauffeur-driven splendour,
> Bearing **charms** no woman could resist!
> In a busy minister's agenda,
> Squeezed one more romantic twist
> With another fellow's wife,
> David led a double life!
>
> And our eyes at last may see him,
> Smitten by a fateful love;
> Fixing tickets; visas for a nanny,
> And who knows what else above!
> But as Blair already stated,
> He will be exonerated!

As with the previous carol, it is essential **before delivery** to briefly revive the audience's memory of the salient elements of associated news item.

While shepherds watched their flocks by night

As even the tragedies in life do **not** escape the attention and exploitation of the humorist, it will come as no surprise to find that the Government's sad mishandling of the B.S.E outbreak in 2001, which led to thousands of cattle having to be slaughtered, again inspired our friend 'Beachcomber' of the Daily Express to come up with more pertinent lyrics for the popular carol 'While shepherds watched their flocks by night'. For maximum impact, and after reminding your audience of the B.S.E. outbreak, be sure **also** to make them aware M.A.F.F. is an acronym for the Ministry of Agriculture, Fisheries, and Food, and that AK 47 rifles were used in the cattle culls.

The lyrics, then, are as follows:

While shepherds **checked** their flocks by night
For foot and mouth disease,
A Minister from M.A.F.F. came down,
And said: 'We'll slaughter these!'

'Fear not,' said he, for mighty dread,
Had seized their troubled mind.
'Our methods really are humane,
And not at all unkind.

'We'll lay down antiseptic mats
At every stile, and gate,
We should have done it months ago;
I'm sorry, that we're late!'

Thus spake the man from M.A.F.F. at farms,
From Durham down to Devon.
An army marksman followed with –
– An AK 47!

Despite the song's humorous aspect, the lyrics could well bring back sad memories for any farmers in your audience, and thus it is always a good idea to follow this with something jolly and light, such as 'The Laughing Taxman'.

The laughing taxman

One of the finest British reciters of saucy songs and dotty ditties was, of course, the late lamented Ronnie Barker, who was also an excellent writer of such material; and as no compendium of such items could ever be deemed representative or complete without a tribute to his wonderful contribution to British comedy, the following item, sung to the tune and rhythm of the well known music hall song by Charles Jolly (the pseudonym of Charles Penrose) called 'The Laughing Policeman', should be a lasting testimonial to his amazing talent:

> I **am** a tax inspector,
> A **jolly** chap, that's me.
> I **deal** with your assessments
> And **drink** a lot of tea!
> You'll **always** find me laughing,
> You'll **never** see me cry,
> I find out **what** you're earning,
> And **then** I bleed you dry!
>
> Oh! A ha-ha, ha-ha, ha-ha-ha etc
>
> I **check** the bills you send me
> I **find out** what you've bought;
> I **look** through your expenses
> Then **cut** them down to nought.
> I **squeeze out** every penny,
> You **all** pay up, like mice,
> And **if** I catch you cheating,
> I **make you** pay up twice!
>
> Oh! Ha-ha etc

I **send** you forms and pamphlets;
It's **fun**, without a doubt,
To **ask** a lot of questions
And **try** to catch you out.
There's **only** one man's tax forms
I **leave there** on the shelf;
Oh yes, I make quite certain
I don't pay tax, myself!

Oh! Ha-ha, etc

When this was performed by the Two Ronnies, there was a pause after the chorus, following which a gun shot was heard – and after a further pause, the words 'Got you, you swine!' rang out. Even if you don't utilise the choruses, which were a feature of the Charles Jolly song, the three main verses above will evoke good audience reaction on their own, as tax is a topic that everyone can identify with!

Don't jump off the roof, Dad

Surprisingly, that wonderful funny man Tommy Cooper, hardly ever featured **comic songs** in his repertoire. Hence it is not commonly known that in 1961, he **did** in fact come out with one called 'Don't jump off the roof, Dad', of which this is a slightly amended, more rhythmical version:

> Daddy came **home** from **work** very tired;
> His **boss** had been **driving him** mad.
> **The kids** were all shouting; **the dog** bit him too;
> His dinner **was nothing** but **a bowl** of cold stew!
>
> **I guess** it was **then** he decided,
> To the **rooftop** now he would go!
> He was **just** about ready to jump off,
> When **the kids** started shouting below!
>
> 'Don't **jump off** the roof just **yet**, Dad,
> **You'll make** a big hole in the yard,
> **Mother's** just planted petunias,
> And the **weeding** and **seeding** was hard!
>
> If you **really** do feel you must end it,
> Won't you **please** now give us a break,
> **Just take** a walk **down** to the park, Dad,
> **As there**, you can jump **into** the lake!'

As it is 46 years since the original version of this song was devised, I have been unable to track down the associated tune. However, liaison with musically minded friends should eventually lead you to a musical number that would suit the rhythm of the lyrics, and in any event, the Tommy Cooper link is sufficient to justify simply reciting it as a 'dotty ditty', if need be.

As time goes by

Another aspect of human life often exploited by humorists is, of course, old age, and hence, when in the company of an audience of mature adults, the following saucy song will certainly strike a few chords and raise plenty of chuckles. Ideally, it needs to be sung to the tune of 'As Time Goes By', which was the theme song to a popular BBC TV comedy programme, featuring Geoffrey Palmer and Judi Dench:

> You **must**, remember this:
> If your **knees** begin to twist,
> And your **thighs do** make you sigh,
> Your **bones** are getting **weaker** now,
> As time goes by.
>
> And **when** you bill and coo,
> But **can't think** of what to do,
> Be **sure** that you **give** it a try,
> The **funda**mentals still apply,
> As time goes by.
>
> Should your **hip joints** then come loose
> And your **heart valves** need a boost,
> Don't try **to be** a talker;
> Just **sip some** Johnny Walker,
> As time goes by.
>
> **Although** that may be risky,
> By **making** you feel frisky,
> Be sure **to en-joy** the thrill,
> Followed **by** a **sleeping** pill,
> As time goes by.

When the **grandkids** pass the bed,
And **to them** you **look** quite dead,
They **never will** query why,
As they **know** some **day** you'll die,
As time goes by.

It's still the **same** old story,
You **never** get the glory,
As **when** they have **read** your will,
They'll be glad **you took** the pill,
As time goes by.

At least you'll be in Heaven,
Having lived to eighty seven,
Now free of all **worldly** pain,
Knowing love **was not** in vain,
As time goes by!

All things bright and beautiful

Most folk have heard the old cliché to the effect that 'the lot of a policeman is **not** a happy one'. Well, at times the same sentiment can also apply to those addicted to gardening, as the following saucy offering drolly confirms. It is best sung to the tune of C.F. Alexander's well known children's hymn 'All things bright, and beautiful':

> All things bright and beautiful, all creatures great and small;
> All things wise and wonderful – the Lord God made them all.
> But what they never mention, though **gardeners** know it's true,
> Is when He made the **goodies**, He made the **baddies** too!

> All things spray and swattable; disasters great and small;
> All things paraquatable, the Lord God made them all!
> The greenfly on the roses; the club root on the greens;
> The slugs that eat the lettuce and chew the aubergines!

> The drought that kills the fuchsias; the frost that nips the buds;
> The rain that drowns the seedlings; the blight that hits the spuds;
> The midges and mosquitos; the nettles, and the weeds;
> The pigeons in the green stuff; the sparrows on the seeds!

> The fly that gets the car-rots; the wasps that eat the plums;
> How black the gardener's outlook, though green may be his thumbs.
> But still, we gardeners labour midst vegetables and flowers;
> And pray what hits our neighbours' may somehow bypass ours!

As a brief though pertinent follow-up, you could mention that even the clergy are not exempt from gardening failures, as confirmed by the following limerick:

> The indolent Vicar of Bray
> Let his roses fall into decay;
> But his wife was alert
> And bought him a squirt,
> Then said to her spouse: 'Let us (s)pray!'

But I don't think it was the Vicar of Bray who said:

> I wish I were a caterpillar,
> Life would be a farce;
> I'd climb up all the flowers and trees
> And slide down on my... hands and knees!!

– not something crude rhyming with 'farce', as most listeners will be expecting you to say!

All things dull and ugly

As comedy/humour has to cater for all tastes, you will have already noticed that even children's songs like 'All things bright and beautiful' can suffer the attentions of the satirist – as the following version of that song, in true Monty Python flavour, again confirms:

> All things dull and ugly,
> All creatures short and squat;
> All things rude and nasty,
> The Lord God made the lot!
>
> Each little snake that poisons;
> Each little wasp that stings;
> He made their brutish venom;
> He made their horrid wings!
>
> All things sick and cancerous;
> All evil great and small;
> All things foul and dangerous,
> The Lord God, made them all!
>
> Each nasty little hornet;
> Each beastly little squid,
> Who made the spiky urchin;
> Who made the sharks? He did!
>
> All things scabbed and ulcerous;
> All pox both great and small;
> Putrid, foul and gangrenous;
> The Lord God made them all!

On a different tack, but in similar Monty Python style, is the following ditty:

When I went walking with my uncle Jim,
A man at a stall threw tomatoes at him.
'Tomatoes don't hurt,' said the Judge with a grin;
But, by gum, they do when they're packed in a tin!

On the 7th day of Christmas

Over the years, the traditional Christmas song entitled 'The Twelve Days of Christmas' has been exploited by humorists in various ways (see the version featured later in this book, within the 'Monologue Mirth' section). But for now, here is a short version that will lighten the mood on occasions when the Christmas party host is bemoaning the **downside** of Christmas entertaining:

One way of getting in to it at an appropriate moment would be to sympathetically suggest that not everybody receives the lovely range of gifts that were a feature of 'The Twelve Days of Christmas' – as in my case:

> On the 7th day of Christmas
> My true love sent to me:
> Seven kids a-screaming,
> Six uncles boozing,
> Five maiden aunts,
> Four snoring dads,
> Three burnt pans,
> Two broken jugs,
> And another lot – coming round for tea!

You could also follow that by saying:

> We are born crying;
> We live complaining;
> We die disappointed;
> Happy New Year!

Having introduced a little jocularity into the proceedings, you could wrap it up by reciting this Christmas Epitaph:

There's very little more to say
And though it may look clever,
It really doesn't always pay
To versify for ever!

So like Gibraltar on its rock,
Or Corinth on its Isthmus,
I'll now retreat and take my seat,
And wish you Happy Christmas!

Dotty Ditties

'Dotty ditties' have a place in any entertainer's repertoire, not only because they are a refreshing change from hackneyed jokes, but also due to the fact that whilst one can often anticipate the climax of a **joke** well before that stage is reached, it is not so with **dotty ditties**, especially those of an Irish flavour, which invariably culminate in a most unexpected ending!

As with the 'Saucy Songs', it was not easy deciding which item to start the 'Dotty Ditty' section with, especially in view of the considerable number to choose from; but eventually I decided on 'The call of the wild' because, despite its link with urination, it really does go down well with **any audience** and, as such, is an excellent example of how even a toilet topic can (with subtlety) be woven into an inoffensive and entertaining ditty.

The call of the wild

The inspiration for this was Christopher Matthew's poem of the same name, from his excellent book of golfing verse entitled: 'Summoned by balls', and published by John Murray of London. Good as it is, I have added another ingredient to the second verse, which improves the humorous impact even more, and I can assure you that the ditty always evokes mirth in any company, not just a golfing environment. When introducing it to your audience, you just need to mention that in addition to it exemplifying the plight of an ageing man being 'caught short' on a golf course, the original poem was written in the guise and rhythm of John Masefield's epic poem 'Sea Fever', the first lines of which are:

> 'I must go down to the sea again – to the lonely sea and sky,
> And all I ask is a tall ship, and a star to steer her by.'

The lyrics, then, are as follows:
I must nip off for a pee again; if I don't, I may well die,
And all I ask is a small bush about four or five feet high;
And a clear view, and a quick slash, and a momentary shaking,
And a light wind, and a good zip that's not forever breaking!

I must pop off for a pee again; Mother Nature won't be denied;
And there's nothing more fun than a pee in the sun, as anyone knows who's tried;
And the breeze through the trees brings a sense of ease, as the white clouds float on by,
But for the worm on the dripping fern, it was certainly 'one in the eye'!

I must take care where I pee again, I'd have sworn there was no one near,
There wasn't a soul for miles around; just crows and a distant deer,
But I had to choose the only place on the whole of the ruddy course,
Where the vicar was down on his hands and knees, hunting for balls in the gorse!

As vicars really **do** play golf and really **can** empathise with the plight of the characters in this ditty; and bearing in mind the tasteful manner in which the dialogue is couched, I know that even the most prim of listeners will not be offended by the references to outdoor 'relief'!

Committees

Returning to the real world, we have all met folk for whom membership of a committee has been the only environment in their lives wherein they have been able to feel important. Again, many of us have sat through the tedious waffling that is so often a feature of committee business processing. If you are one such sufferer, then you should be able to inject a little light relief during your next meeting or gig by reciting the following at an appropriate moment:

> Oh, give me your pity – I'm on a committee,
> Which means that from morning till night,
> We attend and amend, and contend and defend,
> Without a conclusion in sight!
>
> We confer and concur; we defer and demur,
> And reiterate all of our thoughts.
> We revise the agenda with frequent addenda,
> And consider a load of reports!
>
> We propose and compose, we suppose and oppose,
> But see points of procedure as fun!
> And though various notions are brought up as motions,
> There's terribly little gets done!
>
> We resolve and absolve, but we never dissolve,
> Since it's out of the question for us.
> What a shattering pity to end our committee,
> Where else could we make such a fuss?

For best audience reaction, you need to recite this item at a brisk pace, as by that means, the repetitious syllable rhyming will become more noticeable and thus achieve greater impact.

I sense that if all committee folk said the following prayer at the start of each day, then committee business would be completed much more quickly and effectively:

Prayer before breakfast

Prevent us, Lord, from being stodgy and hard to stir – like porridge.

Please make us more like cornflakes – 'ready to serve!'

The tale of dear old Flo'

Although the frustrating impact of pests that beleaguer gardening addicts has already been touched on within the 'Saucy songs' section, it is still fair to say that even someone who, despite that, has succeeded in creating a wonderfully colourful garden can still fall foul of being too familiar with the plants and flowers, as was the case of 'dear old Flo':

This is the tale of dear old Flo, who did talk to all her flowers 'cos she thought it made them grow!

> She recited to her ivy,
> To her fennel, ferns and phlox.
> She chatted to her cacti
> In their little window box!
>
> She murmured to her mosses
> And she yammered to her yew;
> She babbled to her basil,
> To her borage and bamboo!
>
> She lectured to her laurels,
> To her lilac and her lime;
> She whispered to her willows
> And tittered to her thyme!
>
> She gossiped with a poppy
> And she prattled to a rose;
> She regaled her rhododendrons
> With a constant stream of prose!
>
> Then suddenly one morning,
> Her plants keeled over dead!
> Which duly caused old Flo to say:
> 'Was it something that I said?'

I'm a maiden of forty

There are many ways of utilising the following ditty to advantage, one of which being that if someone is becoming a bit of a bore due to a fetish for quoting proverbs, you can inject a little humour into proceedings by posing the rhetorical question: 'We have all heard the well known proverb: A bird in the hand is worth two in the bush, but what is a hand in the bird worth?' After a pause, continue by saying: 'Then I'll tell you, but first, I need you to imagine that I am an attractive 40-year-old blonde(!) (that in itself, will create a chuckle, and also focus audience interest), and we'll let **her** explain':

> I am a maiden who is forty,
> And a maiden I shall stay.
> There are some who call me haughty,
> But I care not what they say.
>
> I was running the tombola
> At our church bazaar today,
> And doing it with gusto
> In my normal jolly way.
>
> When suddenly, I knew not why,
> There came a funny feeling,
> Of something crawling up my thigh;
> I nearly hit the ceiling!
>
> A mouse, I thought; how foul, how mean!
> Though exquis–it–ively tickly!
> Quite soon I knew I'd have to scream,
> I'd got to catch it quickly!

I made a grab; I caught the mouse,
Now right inside my knickers.
A mouse, my foot! It was a hand!
You've guessed! It was the vicar's!

The undertaker's wedding

If called upon to entertain or make a speech at a wedding, then this item will both provoke mirth and also emphasise how the undertaker's wedding experience in the ditty is so far removed from the joy of the gathering that you are duly addressing:

> It left me feeling mournful – of that, I can't pretend –
> When at the April wedding of my undertaker friend.
> Pete was married in a graveyard, a most austere place;
> The priest, by force of habit, threw earth up in my face!
>
> The bloke next plot was digging graves and making clouds of dust,
> But when he saw the lovely bride, his eyes did fill with lust!
> Once pronounced as man and wife, the couple felt quite ill,
> As they had come without the money to pay the vicar's bill!
>
> Breakfast was in the mortuary, among corpses warm and cold;
> We had to sit on coffins, not to mention all the mould!
> The wedding cake, by contrast, stood a pristine three foot four,
> But its lofty nine-inch candle soon fell upon the floor!
>
> A lady duly picked it up, and asked where she should stick it;
> A coarse old man said, 'On the cake; unless you want to lick it!'
> My friend's new bride was dressed in black, in keeping with the venue;
> The best man's face was deadpan, like the mutton on the menu!

The formal speeches did drone on, it seemed they'd never end;
But when they did, old Pete shot off – a funeral to attend!
Tho' many times he'd driven his hearse along the wretched road,
His giddy state did cause my friend to lose his precious load!

But not until he'd reached the church was that sad fact found out;
The widow raised the coffin lid, and let out quite a shout!
Pete quickly went back down the road and found the missing stiff,
But once brought back inside the church, it had an awful whiff!

When put back in the coffin, which the curtains did encloak,
The parson duly pushed the button that sent it up in smoke!
Pete dashed back to the mortuary, but got the shock of his life;
The guests had gone, the best man too – and also Pete's new wife!

But there on top of a coffin, she'd left old Pete a note,
And the message it contained brought a lump into his throat!
'Cos although she once had loved him, and that in no small measure,
He had duly killed it, putting business before the pleasure!

So no wonder it left me feeling mournful!

Silver wedding reminiscences

For a droll sequel to 'The undertaker's wedding', you could continue by stating that even Silver Wedding celebrations are not exempt from the unexpected, as at one Silver Wedding party that I attended, the groom (who I shall refer to as George) stunned all the guests by delivering a ditty which actually highlighted his bride's **adverse attributes**, as opposed to all her **virtues**. An amended version thereof now follows:

> It's twenty five years since we tied the knot;
> Why did we do it? I've nearly forgot!
> Jean was then in her prime, and not very old,
> She'd stay gorgeous for ever – or so I was told!
>
> I tell her she's lovely when I feel kind,
> But my doctor then says I must nearly be blind!
> She used to have hair that shone just like gold;
> But now has a wig, which she washes with Bold!
>
> She's had two new hips and her nose has been fixed,
> Then both sets of teeth out; but they got them all mixed!
> She's a lovely complexion before getting in bed,
> Then washes it off and looks just about dead!
>
> Now just look at me, I've not changed a bit;
> But I get a bit tired; do you mind if I sit?
> I've still got some hair on top of my head,
> But I've forgot what to do when we get into bed!
>
> I don't need paint to make my face red;
> Just four or five pints at the local instead.
> But first thing next morning, when I look in the glass,
> And she offers me breakfast, I have to say 'pass'!

When utilising this ditty, it almost goes without saying that it is readily adaptable to other female personages, providing their names are of one syllable, as in 'Jean'.

Fortunately, not all men are like George, though Romeo, in the following ditty, comes a close second:

> 'Twas in a restaurant they met –
> – Romeo and Juliette.
> He hadn't the money to pay the debt,
> So Rome-o'd, what Juli-ette!

An infant prodigy

Changing tack completely, this item is an excellent example of how a dotty ditty can lead listeners down a particular route, before culminating in the unexpected. Hence, if conversation about families and babies is becoming a little tedious, this ditty will certainly prove to be a relieving diversion:

> Two pickpockets met on a subway train, each picking the other's pocket.
> The woman crook got **his** pocket book; the man got **her** diamond locket!
> Admiring each other, they fell in love; they married, but that was worse.
> They wished for a child that could snatch a bag or pilfer a Scotsman's purse!
> Their wish came true; a boy was born; a slick looking, sly-faced mite!
> But alas he had a crippled hand, and fingers that were closed up tight.
> The heartbroken parents hurried the child to a famous specialist,
> And offered him watches and precious gems if he could unclench the fist.
> First thing he did was to tie a string to a wrist watch with jewelled band,
> And waved it steadily back and forth, just over the crippled hand.
> As the fingers opened, the mother and dad began to dance and sing,
> For there in the palm of the baby's hand was the midwife's diamond ring!

Sonia Snell

As the human fascination with the toilet has captured the interests of humorists all over the world, the following ditty was inspired by a lovely Australian lady from Victoria called Rosalee Roberts:

> This is the tale of Sonia Snell,
> To whom an acci-dent, befell.
> It happened, as it does to many,
> When Sonia went to spend a penny!
> She entered in with modest grace
> The prop-erly appointed place,
> Situ-ated at the station;
> And there she sat in meditation,
> Unfortu-nately un-acquainted
> That the seat had just been painted!
> Her ina-bil-ity to rise
> Made poor Sonia real-ise
> (Though she struggled, pulled and yelled)
> That now she was most firmly held!
> Her cries for help quickly brought
> A crowd of ev'ry size and sort.
> She then let out a mournful shout:
> 'Please someone come and let me out!'
> 'Cor blimey!' said an aged porter,
> 'We'll have to soak her off with water!'
> The station master and his staff
> Were both polite and did not laugh.
> The carpenter knew what to do
> And neatly sawed the seat in two,
> Unfortu-nately to then find
> A halo stuck to her behind!
> An ambulance arrived at last
> And, finding Sonia still stuck fast,

Quickly hoisted her on board
And got her to the accident ward.
The surgeon's staff came on parade
To render their immediate aid,
And holding her by feet and head,
Laid her face down upon the bed.
'Well,' said the surgeon, 'I implore –
has someone seen the likes before?'
'Yes,' said a student, unashamed,
'Quite frequently, but never framed!'

Last night, as I lay sleeping

When conversation is focussing interminably on work, and the stress associated with it, a welcome diversion can be achieved by reciting the following:

> Last night as I lay sleeping,
> I died, or so it seemed.
> Then I went to Heaven,
> But 'twas only in my dreams.
>
> I dreamt St. Peter met me
> There at the Pearly Gate,
> And said: 'I'll check your record,
> So stand right there and wait.
>
> I see that you drank whisky,
> And smoked tobacco too.
> In fact, you've done most things
> That a good man shouldn't do!
>
> We can't have people here like you;
> Your life was full of sin.'
> But then he read the last line
> And instead did say: 'Come in'.
>
> He took me to the Big Boss,
> And asked him to treat me well,
> As I'd worked for British Telecom,
> And had already been through Hell!

Obviously, the ditty can be adapted to relate to any employer whose name contains the same syllable rhythm as British Telecom.

Pete the piddling pup

As a follow-up to the earlier ditty, 'The call of the wild', you could introduce this dotty ditty by saying that it isn't just humans who become conspicuous so far as urination is concerned, as the story of 'Pete the piddling pup' will now confirm. As ever, it culminates with an unexpected twist:

> A farmer's dog once came to town; his Christian name was Pete.
> His pedigree was two yards long, his looks were hard to beat!
> And as he trotted down the street, 'twas beautiful to see
> His 'work' on every corner, and also every tree!
> He watered every gateway; he never missed a post;
> For piddling was his masterpiece, and also was his boast!
>
> The city dogs stood looking on in deep and jealous rage,
> To see that simple country dog as piddler of the age!
> Behind him then those city dogs debated what to do;
> They'd hold a piddling contest and show this stranger who!
> They showed him all the piddling posts they knew there were in town,
> Then started out in lots of pubs to wear this stranger down!
>
> But Pete did cope with every trick, in vigour and in vim;
> A thousand piddles, more or less, were all the same to him!
> And on and on went good old Pete, his hind legs kicking high;
> Whilst most were lifting legs in bluff, and piddling nearly dry!
> They sniffed him over one by one; they sniffed him two by two,
> And noble Pete, in high disdain, stood still till they were through!

Having sniffed him over one by one, their praise for him was high,
But when they sniffed him underneath, Pete piddled in their eye!
Then just to show those city dogs he didn't care a damn,
Pete strolled into the grocer's shop and piddled on the ham!
He piddled on the onions and piddled on the floor,
And when the grocer kicked him out, he piddled on the door!

So on and on went good old Pete, he watered every sand hill,
Till all the city dogs were wa-tered to a standstill!
Then Pete an exhibition gave in all the ways to piddle;
Like double drips and single drips, and now and then a dribble!
And all the time this country dog did neither wink nor grin;
Then blithely piddled out of town as he had piddled in!

The city dogs, said: 'So long Pete; your piddling did defeat us,
But no one ever put them wise – that Pete did have diabetes!

Reminiscences of a senior citizens' tea dance

Coming back to the real world, it is also fair to say that ageing, and the aged, provide humorists with an abundance of chuckle-raising material. The following ditty, inspired by that theme, always goes down well with audiences of mature age:

> When it **was** the tea dance, they **were** all there that day;
> Aches and pains **forgotten**, to **dance** the time away.
> **Foxtrots**, quicksteps, watzes – some **slow** and **some** quite nifty,
> Reminding **folk** of how it was, **way back** in 1950!
>
> **Norman** was in the toilet and **strugg-ling** to pee!
> He had **trouble** with his prostate, and **nearly** missed his tea!
> **Eddy** had a new love he'd **met** on Hampstead Heath;
> She **did** a lovely tango but **sadly** had no teeth!
>
> His **latest** fancy footwork nearly **broke** his lover's neck,
> She **mistook** his body swivel, and **ended** up a wreck!
> **Ivy'd** had her hair done and **was ready** for a saunter,
> But the **vindaloo** she'd had for lunch was **coming back** to haunt her!
>
> Flo's **miniskirt** flew up, when **spinning** in the jive;
> She really **shouldn't** have worn a **thong**, so close to eighty five!
> They **had** their tea and cake and chat, **and** a little laugh,
> And gamely **rose** with creaking knees **to face** the second half.
>
> Norman **made it** back in time for **rumba** number one,
> And **though** his rhythm was quite neat, **he'd left** his flies undone!

Vera then fell over in a **massive** crimplene heap;
Bert had indigestion, and **Mabel** fell asleep!

When **last waltz** came, up they got for **Humperdinck's** old tune,
And **then** 'goodbye, good luck, take care – **God willing**, see you soon!'

Senior citizens' blessings

For an ideal follow up to 'Reminiscences of a senior citizens' tea dance', look no further than the following ditty, which will again strike many chords with an audience of mature age:

> A row of bottles on my shelf
> Made me analyse myself.
> One yellow pill I have to pop
> Goes to my heart, so it won't stop!
>
> A little white one that I take
> Goes to my hands, so they won't shake.
> The blue ones that I use a lot
> Make me happy when I'm not!
>
> The purple pill goes to my brain
> An' tells me that I have no pain.
> The capsules tell me not to wheeze,
> Or cough, or choke, or even sneeze!
>
> The red ones, smallest of them all,
> Go to my blood so I won't fall.
> The orange ones, quite big and bright,
> Prevent bad leg cramps in the night!
>
> Such an array of coloured pills,
> Helping to cure all kinds of ills;
> But what I would, now like to know
> Is how each pill knows where to go!

The moral of all this is that there's a lot to be thankful for, if you bother to look for it, which duly explains why I am sitting here thinking how nice it is that wrinkles don't hurt!

Life spans

Continuing the mature age theme, the following ditty should prove to be an interesting diversion, in the sense that it highlights what old age is to other forms of life, whilst yet again featuring an unexpected ending:

>The **horse and mule** live thirty years,
>Without **needing** wines or beers!
>
>The **goat and sheep** at twenty die,
>And **never** taste a scotch or rye!
>
>A **cow** drinks water by the ton,
>And **when** eighteen is nearly done!
>
>The **dog**, at fifteen, packs it in,
>Without the **aid** of rum or gin!
>
>The cat in **milk** and water soaks
>For **twelve** short years, until it croaks!
>
>The modest, **sober,** bone-dry hen
>Lays **eggs** for us, then dies at ten!
>
>Animals **thus** are strictly dry,
>They **sinless** live, and **swiftly** die!
>
>But sinful, **gin-ful**, rum-soaked men
>Do last for **three** score years and ten!
>
>And **lots** of them, not just a few,
>Stay pickled **till** they're ninety two!
>
>So the moral of this tale has to be that:

There are several reasons for drinking,
And one has just entered my head;
If a man cannot drink when he's living,
How the heck can he drink when he's dead?

Times gone by

Returning to senior citizen memories, the following is yet another excursion back into the 'good old days', which will be appreciated by most audiences of a mature age:

> When **I** was a child, things **weren't** all that bad;
> My **mum** stayed at home and **cooked** for my dad.
> The age of technology **hadn't** been born,
> **Meat** was in burgers, not **substitute quorn**!
>
> There was **no** colour telly, **nor** Channel five,
> **No** mobile phones, but we **still** did survive!
> We **travelled** to school on a **rickety** bus,
> With **no** back doors but we **still** didn't fuss!
>
> We had **no** posh car, nor **gas** central heating,
> We sat at the table till **all** finished eating.
> There **were** no MacDonalds, **nor** Burger King,
> **Records** were vinyl and **at least** we could sing!
>
> The **floors** were all lino'd; the **loo** down the yard,
> We **cooked** all our food with a **big** lump of lard.
> **Stewed** breast of lamb fed us **all** for a week,
> And if **sent up** to bed, we **didn't** dare squeak!
>
> There were **no** tumble dryers, **nor** a deep freeze;
> No **video** recorders, or **even** C.D.s.
> **Outside** the back door, on an **old** rusty nail,
> Was the **old** tin bath, **along**side a pail!
>
> **Out** in the yard stood the **old** iron mangle,
> Which **often** as not got the **clothes** in a tangle.
> The **coal** was delivered on **Friday** each week,
> And **chucked** in the coal house, **despite** its bad leak.

Shops all had counters – no **serve it** yourself,
And **everything** needed was **on** the top shelf.
From **adverts** on telly, you **knew** Stork from butter,
And **after** a road sweep, no **leaves** in the gutter!

Though I'll **never** go back to **that** old house,
With its **creaking** stairs and **resident** mouse,
It's **made** me appreciate **what** I've now got:
A house full of **love**, in **quite** a nice spot!

God.com

As technology **is** now here, along with all its operational problems, someone dependent on a computer for a living could well be excused for sending up a prayer along the following lines:

> **Every** single evening, as I **lie** here in my bed,
> This **tiny** little prayer keeps **running** through my head:
> God bless **all** my family, **wherever** they may be.
> Please **keep** them warm and safe from harm, for **they are** close to me.
>
> And **God,** there **is** just **one** more thing I **wish** that **You** could do;
> Don't **think** me bad for asking – please **bless** my **computer** too!
> Now **I know** that it's unusual to **bless** a motherboard,
> But **listen** just a second, and I'll **explain it** to You, Lord.
>
> You **see**, that little metal box holds **more** than odds and ends;
> **Inside** those small compartments rest **so many** of my friends!
> I **know** so much about them by the **kindness** that they give.
> And my **little** grey computer lets me **in** to where they live.
>
> Through **faith** I've learnt to know them, **much** the same as You;
> We've **shared** what life has brought us; **from** that our friendships grew.
> Please **take** an extra minute from **duties** up above,
> To **bless** those in my address book that **is** so full of love.

I **hope** this prayer **indeed** may reach not **one** but **every** friend,
So **bless** each e-mail in-box, **and he** who **does** hit 'send'!
And **when** You view the Heavenly list on **Your** great CD-Rom,
Bless every**one** who says this prayer, **sent up** to God (**dot**) com!

The Lord's prayer (or 'A London Bus Driver's Lament')

In further confirmation of the fact that **all** human activities are **ongoing** targets for exploitation by humorists, it goes without saying that even prayers do not escape such attention! It will thus come as no surprise to readers to learn that instead of using the normal wording of the Lord's prayer ('Our Father, who art in Heaven, hallowed be Thy name, etc.', some humorist unknown to me concocted a version with a very droll London flavour, as follows:

> Our **Farnham, Welsh Harp** in **Hendon,**
> **Holloway** be Thy name.
> Thy **Kingston** come;
> Thy **Wimbledon,**
> In **Erith**, as it is in **Hendon.**
> Give us this **Bray** our **Maidenhead,**
> And forgive us our **Westminsters,**
> As we forgive those who **Westminster** against us,
> And lead us not into **Thames Ditton**
> But deliver us from **Ealing**
> For thine is the **Kingston,**
> The **Tower** and the **Crawley**
> For **Iver** and **Iver,**
> **Crouch End!**

(For an excellent item that utilises as many as 48 words from the vocabulary of Cockney rhyming slang, look up the 'The Sermon' within the 'Monologue Mirth' section.)

Incorporating humour within prayers is fine, so long as the **actual object** of the prayer is not lost. This was very nearly the case twenty or so years ago, when a version of the following prayer was delivered to an assembly of around 500 bankers at an Institute of Bankers dinner by the then Bishop of Warwick. On conclusion of the prayer, instead of the usual solemnity, the gathering actually burst into applause:

Bankers' prayer

'Lord, we thank you for these gifts before us, which are **tokens** of the rich **deposit** You have **invested** for our **withdrawal**, whenever needed.

Help us to **value** it, and use the **interest** for the **benefit** of our community, so that when we are called by the **Divine Auditor** to give an **account** of our stewardship, He will make up any **deficit; write off** our errors, and prompt us to **pay** a most generous **dividend** of gratitude!

Amen.'

The twins

After a taste of Cockney humour, now to the Irish; and I think it is fair to say that no English-speaking nation can quite match the unique quaintness which is such a refreshing feature of the manner in which the Irish use the English language. Alan Bestic – author of 'The Importance of being Irish', summed up that quaintness when asserting that: 'We use far more words than most nations and somewhere along the line, some of them must be witty, even by accident!'

A wonderful example of that wit and quaintness, is the following slightly amended version of H.S.Leigh's remarkable ditty, 'The twins':

In **form** and feature, **face** and limb,
I **grew** so like my brother
That folks got **taking** me for him,
And **each** for one another!
It puzzled **all** our kith and kin
And **reached** a fearful pitch,
For **one** of us was born a twin,
But **not** a soul knew which!

One day, to **make** the matter worse,
Before our names were fixed,
As **we** were being washed by nurse,
We **got** completely mixed;
And **thus** you see, by Fate's decree,
Or **rather**, nurse's whim,
My brother **John** got christened me,
And **I** got christened him!

This **fatal** likeness ever dogged
My **footsteps** when at school,
And I was **always** getting flogged

When **John** it was the fool!
I put this **question** fruitlessly
To **everyone** I knew,
"What **would** you do, if you were me,
To **prove** that **you** were **you**?!"

Our close **resemblance** turned the tide
Of my **domestic** life,
For **somehow** my intended bride
Became my **brother's** wife!
Year after **year** it was the same,
Absurd **mistakes** went on,
And when I **died** the neighbours came
And **buried** brother John!

The Ballad of William Bloat

To introduce this ditty, it is essential to set the scene by mentioning that the story embodied in the forthcoming verses occurred at the time of the First World War. As ever with Irish ditties, it is best delivered with an Irish accent:

> In a mean abode on the Shankhill Road
> Lived a man called William Bloat.
> He had a wife; the curse of his life,
> Who continually got his goat.
> So one day at dawn, with her nightdress on,
> He cut her bloody throat!
>
> With a razor gash he settled her hash,
> And never was crime so quick;
> But the steady drip on the pillow slip
> Of her life blood made him sick;
> And the pool of gore on the bedroom floor
> Grew clotted, cold and thick!
>
> And yet he was glad that he'd done what he had,
> When she lay there, stiff and still.
> But a sudden awe of the angry law
> Struck his soul with an icy chill.
> So to finish the fun, so well begun,
> He resolved himself to kill!
>
> So he took the sheet off his wife's cold feet,
> And twisted it into a rope,
> And he hanged himself from the pantry shelf;
> 'Twas an easy end, let's hope.
> And in the face of death, with his latest breath,
> He solemnly cursed the Pope!

But the strangest turn to the whole concern
Is only just beginnin'.
He went to hell, but his wife got well!
And **she's** still alive and sinnin':
For the razor blade was German made,
But the sheet was Belfast linen!

Widow Malone (inspired by Charles Lever's original poem of the same name)

For an insight into the mind of an Irish woman, you need go no further than the following:

> There was once a widow called Malone,
> Who lived in Ireland, in Athlone,
> Her beauty melted all the hearts
> Of single men from those parts.
>
> So lovely, the widow Malone.
>
> Of lovers she had a full score,
> And wealth they all had galore.
> From the Minister down
> To the Clerk of the Town.
>
> All courted the widow Malone.
>
> But so modest was Mrs Malone,
> That no one could see her alone.
> Though they'd ogle and sigh,
> They could ne'er catch her eye.
>
> So bashful, the widow Malone.
>
> Till Paddy O'Brien from Clare,
> Who for blushing had never a care,
> Put his arm round her waist,
> Plus ten kisses in haste.
>
> And said: 'You're now **my** Mary Malone!'

And the widow they all thought so shy
Never gave a whimper or sigh.
'Oh Paddy,' said she,
'Since you've made so free,

You may marry your Mary Malone.'

There's a moral contained in my song;
And one comfort – it's not very long!
If for widows you could die,
Learn to kiss, not to sigh.

As they're all like Mistress Malone.

The dilemma of Deirdre Flynn

A lovely example of typical Irish subtlety, and yet another that typifies the Irish delight in creating **contradictions,** is one based on Percy French's original ditty entitled 'Ach I dunno', to which I have given the above title. If dear reader, you are a man, then you should introduce this ditty by inviting the audience to imagine that you are a woman – which will get a chuckle on its own:

> I'm always surrounded by lovers
> Since Pa made his fortune in land.
> They come in flocks like the plovers
> For to ask me for me wee hand.
> There's clerks, accountants and teachers;
> Some blonde, and some black as a crow.
> Ma tells me to humour the creatures,
> But for sure, I don't really know!
>
> The Convent is in a commotion,
> To think of me taking a spouse,
> As of that I gave them no notion
> When it came to taking my vows.
> 'Tis a beautiful life, and is quiet,
> And keeps you from going below,
> Yet still, I thought, I might try it.
> But for sure, I don't really know!
>
> I've none but meself to look after,
> And marriage fills me with fears.
> I think I'd have less of the laughter,
> And certainly more of the tears!
> I'll not be a slave like me mother,
> With six of us all in a row.
> Even one little babbie's a bother.
> But for sure, I don't really know!

There's a lad who has taken me fancy,
But I know he's a little bit dim;
And though marriage is terribly chancy,
I think I would try it with him.
He's coming tonight – oh, I tingle,
From the top of me head to me toe!
But I'll tell him I'd rather stay single –
Though for sure, I don't really know!

Johnny Sands

Much **droll** Irish poetry involves the relationships between men and women. 'Johnny Sands' is in similar vein to 'The Twins', as far as the unexpected twist is concerned, and it goes like this:

> A man who's name was Johnny Sands
> Had married Betty Haig,
> And though she brought him gold and lands,
> She proved a terrible plague!
>
> Says **he**: "I will **drown** myself;
> The river, runs below."
> Says **she**: "Pray **do**, you silly elf –
> I wished it, long ago!"
>
> "For fear that I should courage lack
> And try to save me life,
> Pray tie my hands behind my back".
> "**I will,**" replied his wife!
>
> All down the hill his loving bride
> Now ran with all her force
> To push him in; he stepped aside!
> And **she** fell in, of course!
>
> Now splashing, thrashing like a fish;
> "Oh save me, Johnny Sands!"
> "I can't, my dear, though much I wish,
> For **you** have tied **my** hands!"

So hopefully the last five items will have given you a varied insight into Irish ditty quaintness, and some audience tested material that you can put to good use on the occasion of your next St.Patrick's Day, which of course is on March 17th annually!

Alex and her

For a good example of the exploitation of several puns from a single source, the following ditty is quite clever:

> There was a chap who kept a store;
> And although there were some grander,
> He sold his goods to all who came;
> And his name was **Alexander**.
>
> He mixed his goods with cunning hand;
> He was a skilful brander;
> And since his sugar was half sand,
> They called him **Alex-sander**!
>
> He sought his dear one and she came;
> And lovingly he scanned her,
> He asked her if she'd change her name,
> Then ring did **Alex-hand-her**!
>
> 'Oh yes,' said she, with smiling lip,
> 'If I can be commander!'
> And so they formed a partnership,
> And called it **Alex and her**!

Tongue twister

Having seen how puns can be put to droll use in the creation of dotty ditties, the following, whilst not a ditty in itself, is nevertheless an example of how repetitious rhyme in tongue-twister form can also be exploited to generate a little mirth:

What do you call a donkey with one leg?
A wonky donkey!

What do you call a donkey with one leg and one eye?
A winky wonky donkey!

What do you call a donkey with one leg and one eye making love?
A bonky winky wonky donkey!

What do you call a donkey with one leg and one eye, making love while breaking wind?
A stinky bonky winky wonky donkey!

What do you call a donkey with one leg and one eye, making love while breaking wind, and wearing blue suede shoes?
A honky tonky, stinky bonky, winky wonky donkey!

What do you call a donkey with one leg and one eye, making love while breaking wind, wearing blue suede shoes, and playing the piano?
A plinky plonky, honky tonky, stinky bonky, winky wonky, donkey!

Finally – what do you call a donkey with one leg and one eye, making love while breaking wind; wearing blue suede shoes and playing the piano while driving a bus?
Ruddy talented!

But for something which is a **brain**-twister, as opposed to a **tongue**-twister, I now invite you to make some sense out of the following:

A nod is as good as a wink

An inclination of the cranium is as comprehensible as an oscillation of the optic to an equine quadruped, void of its visionary capacities!

The Miser

In the 1920s and 1930s, an entertainer called Billy Bennett made a good living in the Music Halls by delivering a repertoire of burlesque monologues and recitations. He was a down-to-earth Cockney lad whose idea of evening dress was actually to sport a red handkerchief in his top pocket, wear enormously thick boots along with ill-fitting clothes, and that singular image really did make him stand out from the crowd. To give you a hint of his creativity and humour, an updated version of one of his shorter ditties now follows:

> Up in a filthy garret,
> A place of abandoned hope,
> A miser was counting his money:
> The money he'd saved on soap!
>
> Fed up with life's indigestion,
> And down to his last liver pill;
> Age Concern had forgotten him,
> So he sat down to make his will.
>
> He left all his antique pictures
> To a man who had saved his life,
> And what money **he had** he left to himself,
> But the money **he owed** – to his wife!

Certainly not a very nice way of rewarding his long-suffering wife for all the sacrifices she must have made during their marriage together. Accordingly, had the miser ever had to propose a toast to the ladies, he would have probably come up with something like:

Here's to our wives, who fill our lives
With lots of bees and honey.
They share life's shocks and mend our socks,
But don't they spend the money!

Albert's reunion

I could not move on from the good old music hall entertainers without reference to one of the all-time great creators and performers of comic monologues, the legendary Stanley Holloway. Although he was born in **London's** East Ham, way back in 1890, he acquired a knowledge and appetite for the **Yorkshire** dialect, due to being attached to a Yorkshire regiment during the First World War. This duly served him well when reciting the well known monologue 'The Lion and Albert', which was written by his good friend Marriott Edgar in 1932. What isn't so commonly known is that 46 years later, Stanley himself wrote a sequel to that epic, called 'Albert's reunion', which was every bit as good as the more familiar work – as the following lyrics will duly confirm (they are best recited with a Yorkshire accent):

You've heard of Albert Ramsbottom,
And Mrs Ramsbottom, and dad;
And the trouble the poor lion went to,
Trying to stomach the lad.

Now after the lion disgorged him
Quite many a day had gone by;
But the lion just sat there and brooded,
With a faraway look in his eye.

The keepers could do nowt with lion;
He seemed to be suffering pain;
He seemed to be fretting for summat;
And the curl went out of his mane.

He looked at his food and ignored it,
Just gazed far away into space.
When keepers tried forcible feeding,
They got it all back in their face!

And at Mr and Mrs Ramsbottom's,
The same kind of thing had begun,
When trying all sorts of measures,
They couldn't rouse Albert, their son!

Now Mr Ramsbottom got fed up
With trying to please him in vain,
And said: 'If you don't start to buck up,
I'll take you to lion again!'

Now instead of the lad getting frightened,
And starting to quake at the knees,
He seemed to be highly delighted,
And shouted: 'Oh dad, if you please!'

His father thought he'd gone potty;
His mother went nearly insane.
But Albert just stood there and bellowed:
'I want to see lion again!'

Now Mr and Mrs Ramsbottom
Decided the best thing to do
Was to give way to young Albert,
And take him straight back to the zoo!

The moment the lion saw Albert,
'Twere the first time for weeks it had stirred;
It moved the left side of its whiskers,
Then lay on its back and just purred!

And before anybody could stop him,
Young Albert were stroking its paws;
And whilst the crowd screamed for the keepers,
The little lad opened its jaws!

The crowd by this time were dumfounded;
His mother was out to the wide;
But they knew by the bumps and the bulges
That Albert were once more inside!

Then all of a sudden, the lion
Stood up and let out a roar;
And Albert, all smiling and happy,
Came out with a thud on the floor!

The crowd, by this time, were all cheering,
And Albert stood there looking grand,
With his stick with 'orse's 'ead handle,
Clutched in his chubby young hand!

The lion grew so fond of Albert,
He couldn't be parted from lad,
And so the zoological keepers
Sent round a note for his dad!

'We regret to say, lion is worried,
And pining for your little man,
So sending you lion tomorrow,
Arriving in plain covered van!'

And if you call round any evening,
I'll tell you just what you will see:
Albert is reading to lion in bed,
And what is he reading? – 'Born free'!

I take it, you already know

Talking about reading, if conversation ever revolves round how difficult the English language must be for non-English speaking people to learn, due to the pronunciation variations of particular letter groups – such as 'ough', which can be pronounced in eight different ways, eg 'though' ('oh'); 'rough' ('uff'); 'through' ('oo'); 'cough' ('off'); 'thought' ('ort'); 'bough' ('ow'); 'hiccough' ('up'); and 'lough' (as in loch - 'och') – you can add fuel to that via the following ditty:

> I take it you already know
> Of tough, and bough, and cough, and dough?
> Others may stumble, but not you,
> On hiccough, thorough, lough, and through!
> Well done! And now you wish, perhaps,
> To learn of less familiar traps?
> Beware of **heard**, a dreadful **word**,
> That looks like **beard** but sounds like **bird**!
> And **dead** – it's said like **bed**, not **bead**;
> For goodness sake, don't call it **deed**!
> Watch out for **meat**, and **great**, and **threat** –
> They rhyme with **suite**, and **straight**, and **debt**!
> A **moth** is not a moth in **moth**er,
> Nor **both** in **both**er, **broth** and **broth**er!
> And **here** is not, a match for **there**,
> Nor **dear** and **fear**, for **bear** and **pear**!
> And then there's **dose**, and **rose**, and **lose**-
> Just look them up, and **goose**, and **choose**.
> And **cork**, and **work**, and **card**, and **ward**;
> And **font**, and **front**, and **word**, and **sword**;
> And **do**, and **go**, and **thwart**, and **cart**!
> Come, come, I've hardly made a start!
> A dreadful language? Man alive!
> **I'd mastered it** when I was **five**!
>
>   Dream on!

There's no truth in all that at all

An ideal sequel to 'I take it you already know', which highlights the peculiarities of the **names** accorded to animals and other creatures, is as follows:

> The **cheet**ah, my friends, is not known to **cheat**.
> The **tig**er possesses no **tie**.
> The **horse**fly, of course, was never a **horse**,
> And the **li**on did not tell a **lie**!
> The **turk**ey, though perky, was never a **Turk**,
> Nor a **monk**ey ever a **monk**.
> The **man**drill, though like one, was never a **man**,
> But some men are **like** one when drunk!
> The **spring**bok, dear thing, wasn't born in the **spring**;
> The **wal**rus did not build a **wall**.
> No **bad**ger is **bad**; no **add**er can **add**;
> There's no truth in those things at all!

Talking of walls – and after a brief reference to the familiar ditty 'Ten green bottles standing on the wall' – you could lighten the mood a bit more with the following:

> There were ten sticks of dynamite standing on a wall,
> And if one stick of dynamite should accidentally fall,
> There'd be **no** sticks of dynamite, and **no** ruddy wall!

The plaint of the camel

As confirmed in the verse 'There's no truth in all that at all', animals are often a feature of dotty ditties, a prime example of which now follows. If you detect an American flavour, it is because its originator, Charles Edward Carryl, was in fact a successful American writer of the 19th and 20th centuries, who was considered by many to be America's answer to England's Lewis Carroll! The word 'plaint' is used in the context of a grievance, and thus the lyrics are as follows:

> Canary birds feed on sugar and seed;
> Parrots have crackers to crunch;
> And as for the poodles, they tell me the noodles
> Have chickens and cream for their lunch!
> But there's never a question
> About my digestion;
> Anything does for me!
>
> Cats, you're aware, can repose in a chair;
> Chickens can roost upon rails;
> Puppies are able to sleep in a stable,
> And oysters can slumber in pails!
> But no one supposes
> A poor **camel** dozes;
> Any place does for me!
>
> Lambs are **en**closed where it's never **ex**posed,
> Coops are constructed for hens;
> Kittens are treated to houses well heated,
> And pigs are protected by pens!
> But a **camel** comes handy
> Wherever it's sandy,
> Anywhere does for me!

People would laugh if you rode a giraffe
Or mounted the back of an ox;
It's nobody's habit to ride on a rabbit,
Or try to bestraddle a fox!
But as for a **camel**, 'e's
Ridden by fam-il-ies;
Any load does for me!

A snake, is as round as a hole in the ground,
And weasels are wavy and sleek;
And no alligator could ever be straighter
Than lizards that live in a creek.
But a **camel**'s all lumpy,
And bumpy, and humpy,
Any shape does for me!

The new ABC's

'The plaint of the camel' in the previous ditty is nothing compared to the human suffering embodied in the following novel ditty/dialogue:

A is for apple, and **B** is for boat
That **used** to be right but **now** it won't float.
Age before beauty is **what** we once said,
But **if** I am truthful and **realistic** instead,
then:

A's for arthritis; **B**'s a bad back;
C is for chest pains, perhaps cardiac;
D is for dental, decay and decline;
E is for eyesight, can't read the top line;
F is for fissures, and fluid retention;
G is for gas; which I'd rather not mention;
H is high blood pressure; I wish mine was low;
I for incisions, with scars you can show;
J is for joints out of socket, won't mend;
K is for knees that crack when they bend;
L for libido, when much oversexed;
M is for memory; I've forgotten what's next!
N's for neuralgia, in nerves way down low;
P's for prescriptions; I **have** quite a few;
Just **give** me a pill and I'll **be** good as new.
Q is for queasy; is it fatal, or 'flu'?
R is for reflux – one meal becomes two;
S is for sleepless, counting my fears;
T is for tinnitus; there's bells in my ears!
U is for urine; big troubles with flow;
V is for vertigo – that's dizzy, you know!
W is for worry, now what's going round;
X is for x-ray and what might be found;

Y is another year that I've left behind;
Z is for zest; which is still in my mind!

I've survived all the symptoms, my body's deployed,
Keeping twenty six doctors fully employed!

Little Red Riding Hood and the Big Bad Wolf (adult version!)

When folk are reminiscing about their childhood days and bemoaning the fact that there are no longer any good fairy stories being written for young people, such as Little Red Riding Hood, you could interject by suggesting that there has merely been a change of emphasis, in the sense that fairy stories are **now** being written with the needs of adults in mind. A good example of this is the adult version of: 'Little Red Riding Hood and the Big Bad Wolf':

> As soon as Wolf began to feel
> That he would like a decent meal,
> He went and knocked on Grandma's door,
> And when she opened it she saw,
> The sharp white teeth, the horrid grin,
> And Wolfie saying: 'May I come in?'
>
> Poor Grand-ma-ma was terrified;
> 'He's going to eat me up!' she cried;
> And she was absolutely right –
> He ate her up in one big bite!
> But Grand-ma-ma was small and tough,
> And Wolfie wailed: 'That's not enough!'
>
> 'I haven't yet begun to feel
> That I have had a decent meal!'
> He ran around the kitchen, yelping:
> 'I've **got** to have another helping
> Then added with a frightful leer:
> 'I'm therefore going to wait right here,

Till Little Miss Red Riding Hood
Comes home from walking in the wood!'
He quickly put on Grandma's clothes;
(Of course, he hadn't eaten those!)
He dressed himself in coat and hat;
He put on shoes, and after that,

He even brushed and curled his hair
Then sat himself in Grandma's chair.
In came the girl, all dressed in red,
She stopped and stared, and then she said:

'What big ears you have, Grandma!'
'All the better to hear you with,' the Wolf replied.
'What big eyes you have, Grandma!' said Little Red Riding Hood.
'All the better to see you with,' the Wolf replied.

He sat there watching her and smiled.
He thought, 'I'm going to eat this child;
Compared to her old Grand-ma-ma,
She's going to taste like caviare!'

Little Red Riding Hood, duly said:
'But Grandma, what a lovely great big furry coat you have on!'
'That's wrong!' cried Wolf; 'Have you forgot
To tell me what big teeth I've got?'

'Ah well, no matter what you say,
I'm going to eat you anyway!'
The small girl smiles; one eyelid flickers;
She whips a pistol from her knickers,
And aims it at the creature's head,
Then *bang, bang, bang,* she shoots him dead!

A few weeks later, in the wood,
I came across Miss Riding Hood;
But what a change; no cloak of red,
No silly hood upon her head.
She said: 'Hallo, and do please note,
My lovely, furry, **wolf**skin coat!'

William the Conqueror

To further emphasise that humour is all-embracing is the fact that it can even be utilised within the world of education, in order to make the learning of some topic more palatable to pupils. Hence, after reciting the following, no one can be in any doubt as to the period in which William the Conqueror reigned:

> William the Conqueror in 1066
> Said to his Captains: 'I mean to affix
> England to Normandy. Go out and do borrow
> Some bows and some arrows; we're starting tomorrow'.
> So William went conquering, hither and thither
> Till Angles and Saxons were all of a dither.
> He conquered so quickly, you couldn't keep count
> Of the countries he conquered; I think they amount
> To ten, or a dozen, or even a score,
> And I haven't a doubt he'd have conquered some more.
> So full and so proud of his conquering tricks,
> Was William the Conqueror of 1066!
> But death put an end to the tactics, thank heaven,
> Of William the Conqueror in 1087

The toilet testament

Closely linked to the theme of the Epilogue's thesis on 'Fartology' is this dotty prayer, featuring the frustrations encountered within 'the room where there is only one seat' – i.e. the toilet(!). As it is tastefully written, it will strike many a chord with most audiences:

> Bless **this room**, oh Lord, we pray;
> Make it **sweet** by night and day.
> Bless **the seat** and bless the flush
> Bless the early morning **rush**!
> Bless the nasty little **brat**
> Who pulled the **chain** and drowned the **cat**!
> Bless the girl **who locked** the door,
> And sat there **reading** for evermore!
> Bless the phantom's **dirty feet**,
> The prints of whom are on the **seat**.
> Bless the guy who thought he ought-er
> Try a taste of **toilet water**!
> Bless the fiend, whose fav'rite **caper** –
> To leave you stranded with **no paper**!
> Finally, with **love and kisses**,
> Bless the fool who **always misses**!

A mother's lament

From the frustrations of the toilet to those of a mother whose offspring appeared to be vanishing before her very eyes! This ditty is a development of what I believe originally began as a **song**, but like so many bits of business one comes across from time to time, I am unable to give the originator of that song credit, as I have no idea who he/she was! In any event, the restructured version that follows is intended to be recited merely as a **dotty ditty**, and is appropriate to occasions when mothers and babies are the topic of the moment:

> A mother was bathing her baby one night;
> The youngest of ten, a tiny wee mite.
> The mother was poor and the baby was thin;
> Only a skeleton covered with skin!
> The mother turned round for the soap off the rack,
> She was but a moment; but when she looked back,
> Her baby was gone: and in anguish she cried:
> 'Oh, where is my baby?' – the angels replied:
>
> 'Your baby has gone down the plughole;
> Your baby has gone down the plug.
> The poor little thing was so skinny and thin,
> It should have been washed in a jug!
> Your baby is ever so happy,
> He won't need a bath any more,
> As he's playing about with the angels above,
> Not lost, but just gone before!'
>
> The mother was frantic; the baby was gone,
> But she still had nine more and the water was warm.
> She covered her eyeballs and stuck in a pin;
> Picked out another babe, ever so thin,
> Then into the water; she brushed off a tear,

But when she looked up, cried: 'Crumbs, it's not here;
Now that one's gone!', and in anguish she cried:
'Oh, where is my baby?' – the angels replied:

(repeat second verse)

The mother was livid; 'How dare you?' she cried.
'Don't take no more chances,' the angels replied.
'We've had your two young'ns; we'd like a few more!'
Then gave a nice smile and dissolved through the floor!
Now mother was boiling; she smashed in the bath.
'You're not having my kids!' she cried with a laugh.
'They've not touched no water, from that very day,
'It's the smell,' mother says, 'that keeps angels away!'

Delivering this with a northern accent will further strengthen its comic impact on your audience.

The Ballad of Bethnal Green (inspired by Paddy Roberts)

Paddy Roberts was a successful British musical movie **song writer** of the 1950s, and like the previous item, 'A mother's lament', what now follows in dittyfied form was inspired by Paddy's song of the above title:

> I'll tell a tale of a jealous male, and a maid of sweet sixteen.
> She was blonde and dumb and she lived with her mum on the edge of Bethnal Green.
> She worked all week for a rich old Greek; her old man was on the dole;
> And her one delight on a Friday night was a session of rock and roll.
>
> Then one fine day in the month of May, she found her big romance,
> He was smart, and sleek with a scar on his cheek, and a pair of drainpipe pants!
> And she thought: 'With you, I could, be so true, through all the years to come',
> For she loved the gay, abandoned way he chewed his chewing gum!
>
> It started well because he fell for all her girlish charms,
> But he had some doubt when he caught her out in someone else's arms
> And he said: 'Look here, you know, my dear, this is going a bit too far',
> And went quite white as he sloshed her right in the middle of her cha cha cha!

So he went before a man of the law, who said: 'This will not do.
'I've had about enough of this kind of stuff as I want from the likes of you.'
And she was peeved, when he received, a longish term in clink,
And in a fit of pique she married the Greek, and now she lives in mink!

As a quick follow up to that, you could suggest to your audience that if you met such a lady at the bus stop, you would be tempted to say:

Oh come with me and be my love,
I keep a flat for mating.
There's half an hour before the bus;
Shall we do it while we're waiting!

Merry Christmas, you suckers

As a sequel to 'Away in a manger' in the 'Saucy Song' section, you could introduce this item by suggesting that although Christmas is meant to be a happy time, there are always some, like Dickens' Scrooge in 'A Christmas Carol', who dwell on the miserable side of life. What you are about to read is a dittified version of a song inspired by the redoubtable Paddy Roberts:

> Merry Christmas, you suckers; you miserable men;
> That old festive season is with us again!
> You'll be spending your money on cartloads of junk,
> And from here to New Year you'll be drunk as a skunk!
>
> Merry Christmas, you suckers, it's perfectly clear
> That you fall for it all a bit sooner each year!
> If it goes on like this, you'll find pretty soon
> That you're singing 'White Christmas' as early as June!
>
> This Christmas card racket will cost you a packet,
> Each season it seems to expand;
> The cards are so clever, though nothing whatever
> To do with the subject at hand!
>
> You'll be taking the kids round the multiple stores,
> To be frightened to death by an old Santa Claus
> Then its parties with spirits and vino and beer,
> Merry Christmas, you suckers, and a Happy New Year
>
> Merry Christmas, you suckers; you bleary-eyed lot;
> You'll never get rid of the headache you've got!
> But I hope you'll feel splendid you certainly should,
> With your stomachs distended with turkey and pud!

Merry Christmas, you suckers; jump into your cars;
Roar off to your neighbours' to sink a few jars.
Though your vision is double just keep smiling through,
There are others in trouble a lot worse than you!

Beyond any question, acute indigestion
Will plague you and make you unwell.
You won't take the warning; you'll wake up each morning
Undoubtedly feeling like hell!

But stick to it suckers; go swallow a pill,
For this is the season of peace and goodwill.
While we patiently wait for that nuclear blast,
Merry Christmas, you suckers, it may be your last!

Santa's lament

Although the traditional image of Santa Claus is that of a red-suited, white-bearded, happy-faced, generous old man who children love to meet, the truth is that just like normal people, Santa sometimes becomes fed up with it all, as is the case in the following ditty of unknown origin:

> 'Twas the night before Christmas, old Santa was whacked.
> He cursed all the elves and told them: 'You're sacked!
> Miserable little brats; ungrateful little jerks;
> I've a good mind to scrap the whole ruddy works!'
>
> 'I've worked off my backside for nearly a year,
> And instead of "Thanks, Santa", what do I hear?
> The old lady gripes 'cos I work late at night;
> The elves want more money; the reindeer all fight!
>
> Rudolph got drunk and raped all the maids;
> Donner is pregnant and Blitzen has Aids;
> And just when I thought that things would get better,
> The damn Inland Revenue sent me a letter!
>
> They say I owe taxes; that's got to be funny;
> As no one has ever sent Santa some money!
> And tho' children these days receive loads and loads,
> They still ask for more, the mean little toads!
>
> I've spent the whole year making bunnies and teds;
> And fitting up dolls with arms, legs and heads.
> I've made loads of yo-yos; but no call for them,
> It's computers they want, from old I.B.M.

Flying through snowflakes and dodging the trees;
Falling down chimneys and scraping my knees;
I'm quitting the job; there's just no enjoyment,
So I'll sit on my backside and draw unemployment!

No Christmas this year, but not for that reason;
I'm off south with a blonde for the rest of the season!

The Illusionist's assistant

As Christmas is a magical time in many ways, what follows is a droll ditty linked to the world of real magic that was put together by English magicienne Rachel Wild. It **conjures up (!)** a word picture of what it must be like climbing in and out of wooden boxes on stage every night! Rachel has since married Italian-American magician, Aldo Colombini.

Her outfit, sleek and sparkling;
Her shape, quite small and thin;
Not weighing more than 90lbs,
There's a box she must fit in!

Sequins, heels and makeup
That look great when she's on stage
Do hide a multitude of sins,
The main one being her age!

Dancing lessons are a must,
If she wishes to impress,
But if she really cannot dance,
She wears a skimpy dress!

Her audience will soon notice,
They are easy to distract;
She'll be who they're looking at,
Not her partner's magic act!

She'll squeeze inside the little cube,
Her big toe in her ear!
The music will be very loud;
So her cries they will not hear!

She'll try to exit gracefully
With a big run in her hose;
Her thong then cutting into her,
As she holds her final pose!

She vows to get a real job,
With benefits and good pay;
But with the audience cheering,
She'll stay for one more day!

Today I'm 80

For a sequel to 'As time goes by' in the 'Saucy Song' section, the following dotty ditty, of unknown origin to me, may sound familiar to some, up to the verse featuring the age of 89. But thereafter, most will find it refreshingly new:

> Today, dear lord, I'm 80,
> And there's much I haven't done.
> So I hope, dear Lord, you'll let me
> Live till I'm 81!
>
> But then if I haven't finished
> All I want to do,
> Please let me stay awhile,
> At least till 82!
>
> To many a place I want to go;
> So very much to see,
> So could you possibly manage
> To make it 83?
>
> The world is changing very fast;
> There is so much to live for,
> So if it's quite alright with you,
> I'll go at 84!
>
> By then a cruise is on the cards,
> So if I'm still alive,
> With so much more to follow,
> Could I stay till 85?
>
> More planes to take me through the air;
> So I'd really like to stick
> And see what happens to the world
> When I'm 86!

I know, dear God, it's much to ask,
And it must be nice in Heaven,
But I really would like to stay
Until I'm 87!

I know by then I won't be fast,
And sometimes will be late,
But it really would be pleasant
To be around at 88!

I will have seen so many things
And had a marvellous time,
So I'm sure I'll be willing
To leave at 89!

Well maybe; just may be!
But still, I don't feel ready,
To fin-al-ly let go
And miss the super party
For my really big 9-0!

Lord, please don't think me greedy
For wanting some more fun;
But please could you allow me
To live till 91!

And if I really do behave
And there's several in the queue,
Perhaps you could allow me
To stay till 92!

An even nicer number,
I am sure that you'll agree,
Is yet another challenge –
To live till 93!

Once I reach the 'Pearly Gates'
And am standing at the door,
Should you still be busy,
I'd stay till 94!

Such an age I'd bear with pride,
So glad to be alive,
But I'd even be much prouder
To live till 95!

By then with every dawning day,
I'd watch the hall clock tick,
And wouldn't miss a single second
Till reaching 96!

Although I know that your plan
Was to bring me into Heaven,
But could you kindly save my seat,
Until I'm 97?

By then I would still stick around
Much closer to your Gate;
Just in case you ever thought
I'd not make 98!

I know my body cannot last
And will soon be in decline,
But I really want to drag it on
Until I'm 99!

Though my life has not been perfect,
And indeed I've often blundered;
Pray let me get my telegram
By living till a hundred!

I'm fine, thank you!

When considering dotty ditties featuring an 'old age' theme, it seemed only right to ensure that this lovely creation be preserved for posterity, despite it being a quite well worked ditty, and the author also being unknown:

> There is nothing the matter with me;
> I'm as healthy as can be.
> I have arthritis in both my knees,
> And when I talk, I talk with a wheeze.
> My pulse is weak and my blood is thin,
> But I'm awfully well for the shape I'm in!
>
> Arch supports I have for my feet,
> Or I wouldn't be able to walk on the street.
> Sleep is denied me, night after night,
> But every morning I find I'm alright.
> My memory's failing; my head's in a spin,
> But I'm awfully well for the shape I'm in!
>
> The moral of all this, my tale I unfold,
> That for you and me, who are growing old,
> It's better to say: 'I'm fine' with a grin,
> Than to let folks know the shape we are in!
>
> How do I know that my youth is all spent?
> Well, my 'get up, and go' has got up and went!
> But I really don't mind when I think with a grin
> Of all the grand places my 'get up' has been!
>
> Old age is golden, I've heard it said,
> But sometimes I wonder as I get into bed
> With my ears in a drawer, my teeth in a cup,
> My eyes on the table until I wake up.

Till sleep overtakes me, I say to myself:
'Is there anything else I could lay on the shelf?'

When I was young, my slippers were red;
I could kick my heels over my head.
When I was older, my slippers were blue,
But I could still dance the whole night through.
Now I am old, my slippers are black,
I walk to the shops and puff my way back!

I get up each morning and sharpen my wits,
And pick up the paper and read the 'Obits'.
If my name is missing, I know I'm not dead,
So I have a good breakfast and go back to bed!

Balanced viagra

Whilst on the topic of old age, and ageing men in particular, you can have a lot of fun with this, my much altered and 'dittyfied' version of a Caribbean calypso type song, called 'Viagra', which is one of fifteen songs of similar style and rhythm on a C.D. called 'The Barefoot Man'. Although offered here as a dotty ditty, if you can impersonate the native Caribbean voice and rhythm, it is certainly worth endeavouring to find a tune to go with it, as that will further enhance your performance.

> **Viagra, viagra, viagra,**
> This **won**derful, **mag**ical pill;
> Fill up **our jars** with viagra,
> It's **time** old **boys** had a thrill!
>
> Well **Tom** – he got a prescription,
> For this **amazing** sexual pill,
> In **order** to **help** his condition,
> As he **was** well **over** the hill!
>
> But **Tom** he **took** a few extra,
> And **said** to himself: 'What the heck'.
> But **though** his **girl** he did pamper,
> All he **got** was a **very** stiff neck!
>
> When **Harry** did call his G.P.
> To **tell him** viagra don't work,
> He was **told** to take it with tea,
> And **not** to be **such** a great berk!
>
> When **at last** it **had** an effect,
> His **wife** became **shocked** by the size;
> But **after** a while to reflect,
> She **quickly** did **close up** her thighs!

As **sex** was no **fun** with his 'Honey',
His **jar** he chucked **into** the bin,
Thinking it **waste** of good money,
He **won't** use **viagra** again!

His **dog** duly **found** Harry's jar,
And he **swallowed** viagra somehow,
Then **chased** ev'ry bitch from afar,
And is **more** like a **rottweiler** now!

Now **Dick** was a **bald**-headed fella,
And his **brain** was **on** a go slow,
But he'd **heard** that magic viagra,
Could **make** almost **anything** grow!

So **he emptied** his jar of viagra,
And **rubbed it** all **over** his head,
His **hair** grew **like** a tiara,
But the **rest** of him **looked** about dead!

Some **folk** they **do** need viagra,
Or **sev'ral** new **antics** to try.
Some like the **thrill** of Niagara,
Or a **drink** to **help** them get by!

Some **folk**, they **need** a vibrator
To **give** them a **boost** to their life,
But **I** don't **need** the viagra,
'Cos **I've got** a **beautiful** wife!

Mary had a little lamb

No compendium of dotty ditties could ever be deemed adequately representative without a sample of those featuring the familiar first line: 'Mary had a little lamb'. So to kick-start the following selection, here is one inspired by the 90-year-old *Daily Express* journalist 'Beachcomber'. It is actually an ideal sequel to 'While shepherds watched their flocks by night' in the 'Saucy Song' section, as it drolly reminds us of the meat price fluctuations caused by the handling of the devastating B.S.E. outbreak of 2001:

> Mary had a little lamb;
> It gave her indigestion,
> But at its price, to serve up beef
> Was really out of the question!
>
> 'But I remember,' Mary said,
> 'When beef was almost free!'
> But mother sighed and then replied:
> 'That was due to B.S.E.!'
>
> 'They slaughtered all the cows, you see;
> You could not move for meat,
> Butchers dropped the price to zilch
> To make our Sunday treat'.
>
> 'But then the price shot up again;
> So now we're eating sheep,
> For breakfast, dinner, lunch and tea;
> Monotonous, but cheap!'

Now for a couple that are more conventional in style and theme:

Mary had a little lamb;
She also had a bear,
I've often seen her little lamb,
But I've never seen her bare!

Mary had a little lamb,
Cold custard and some prunes;
A pint of ale, a sip of gin,
And a plate of macaroons!

She also ate some apple tart
And a little sturgeon's roe;
But when they carried Mary out,
Her face was white as snow!

A view of cruising

When it comes to comic verse, dear old Pam Ayres takes some beating; hence, after coming across a droll poem she wrote for charity while aboard a major cruise liner in 2005, I was inspired to write a more general version thereof that didn't specify any particular ship:

> I'm on a lovely liner, she's beautiful and so strong;
> Her décor so exquisite, and her passages oh so long!
> I feel a grand excitement as the band begins to play,
> And she casts off all her ropes, and starts to sail away.
>
> So as I cruise on this big ship in luxury and ease,
> It slips past many islands amid the seven seas,
> And by some naval magic, it always keeps on track
> But if I leave the cabin, I can't tell the front from back!
>
> The motion of the vessel and the rolling of the sea;
> And the moonbeam on the ocean is paradise to me.
> Plus the magic of the planet, and brightness of the sun,
> But the awesome cabin toilet can hardly be called fun!
>
> I had a little fracas when unpacking all the clothes;
> A woman needs much hanging space, as everybody knows,
> But all was soon resolved and with harmony once more;
> The wife got thirty hangers, and I settled for one drawer!
>
> When I think of this big ship, it's the speed that I love most,
> But for many others, it's the food that is their boast.
> Still more do like to tell you of the cruises they've been on,
> Whilst some bemoan the fact that of credit they had none!

But oh that force eleven; gigantic waves and more;
The teaspoons and the crockery all shoot across the floor!
If seasick in your cabin, you'll be helpless and quite weak,
And items like the wardrobe will have a haunting creak!

I love the sunny mornings, and I love the humid nights,
The kindness of the stewards, and the Captain in his whites.
But what could be more soothing that to spend a pleasant hour,
Together with your true love in the cabin shower!

There are very many things to do while the ship's at sea,
But a visit to the laund'rette is really, not for me,
As if you take some washing out that's not in fact your own,
You'll be the victim of some insults, and a broken bone!

But now it's time to say goodbye from me, your friend, who cares,
And even if you see again the sick bags on the stairs,
Take a crumb of comfort as you go to sleep at night,
You could be back in Blighty, and not a pretty sight!

Life on a cruise ship

For a more in-depth insight into the vagaries of cruising, the following dotty ditty will strike chords with readers who are already familiar with that form of holiday experience. It is based on one written some time ago by a fellow passenger whose name escapes me:

> This cruising lark is so much fun,
> Not just for us but everyone;
> With cocktail parties full of glitz,
> And endless flow of gin and its!
>
> The Captain smiles and shakes your hand,
> Then says: 'Bah gum – you're looking grand!'
> 'Cos he's from Wigan – born and bred,
> No frills on him, it must be said!
>
> The officers there, so young and gay,
> Chat up the ladies as they stray,
> And though they've heard it all before,
> Each cruise they still come back for more!
>
> The gents, all dressed like tailors' dummies,
> With trousers tight around their tummies;
> Each strutting about like some toff,
> Yet yearning to get the damn things off!
>
> Next day on deck you'll hear the cry:
> 'Join in the quoits, and have a try
> To win a prize – no, not a cruise;
> A notebook, yes, but oh, no booze!'

Yet you really can win some fizz,
By joining a team for the quiz,
And should, by chance, you reach the top,
Then your champagne cork will go pop!

For arty folk who love to paint,
And think they're Rembrandt but they ain't,
They learn it takes much more, than guile
To emulate a Master's style!

For those inclined to go on line,
The cyber study suits them fine,
But sadly, systems often fail,
So those back home, get no e-mail!

For those no longer in a trance,
There is a chance to learn to dance,
All shapes and sizes take the floor,
Then come off aching and footsore!

The cruise soon passes, like a dream,
More friends made and new sights seen,
And though it's great to sample Rome,
There's really still no place like home!

Shuffleboard aboard

In what has been, in a sense, a trilogy of cruise-flavoured dotty ditties, this final one specifically centres on the popular (but very competitive!) deck game called 'Shuffleboard'. The narrative takes place in a bar called the Masquerade, where participants regularly meet, after the games. The original version was written by a passenger, who sadly I only know as Roger:

> Well, here we are in Masquerade,
> To meet the friends that we have made
> At shuffleboard, that game of skill,
> Of smiling faces – and looks that kill!
>
> We like to say it's just for fun,
> But if you lose, pass me that gun!
> Although the ones we see as wise,
> Don't really want to win a prize!
>
> We stoop and gently push the puck,
> We pray for just a slice of luck,
> But book your deckchair straight away,
> If on Court 4 you have to play!
>
> Most of us are out first time,
> We smile and say it's not a crime,
> 'Did you play well?' 'Oh yes,' we say,
> 'My partner threw the game away!'
>
> You try to help your partner through,
> 'You pushed too hard!' she screams at you.
> It is my friend; oh what a girl,
> The one and only lovely Pearl!

Moans, and cheers; cries of pain,
Alex's bloody stupid game;
You hear that OO AH OO, an' then:
Someone's got, a minus 10!

'You're in the semi-final, son!'
'Thanks, mate – now the pressure's on'.
The final puck is straight or bend,
You wish that you could phone a friend!

Deckchairs neatly in a row,
Must be for the final show,
Iris isn't there to play,
Roger let her down today!

Near the end the players huddle;
Is the scorer in a muddle?
Who has won the key and pen?
Of course, it's Tony once again!

Fin-ally, a word or two,
About, the enter-tainment crew.
Paragons of charm, and yet,
Pens and score sheets they forget!

'I'll take your names in just a trice,
Ladies first – I've told you twice!'
But just a plea to those who know,
Those tatty prizes have to go!

So that's the morning gone and then
In just two hours, we start again,
But it's the game we love to play,
With friends and foes each sunny day!

So when you are back home again,
Looking at the pouring rain,
Think of that great final when
Your final puck went in, plus ten!

Ship-shape

Though not dotty in itself, the nautical flavour of this next ditty (of unknown origin) and the truisms contained in it made me feel it was worthy of inclusion in this compendium:

> The sea of life presents us
> With some currents that confuse,
> And many '**ships**' are needed
> On any type of cruise.
>
> Apprentice-**ship** and Workman-**ship**
> Can form a worthy crew,
> Leader-**ship** and Statesman-**ship**,
> Can help to steer us through.
>
> Wor-**ship** is a Flag-**ship**
> That is care-fully designed,
> And proper navigation
> Can leave Hard-**ship** far behind!
>
> Though the sea of life's uncharted,
> At times it must be said:
> The finest craft is Friend-**ship**
> When it steams full speed ahead!

Jack Sprat for grown-ups

In any company, there are always some folk who let it be known that they abhor fat or overweight people, and in such a situation, you can come to the aid of the latter by mentioning that in the grown-up version of the nursery rhyme involving Jack Sprat, overeating actually proved to be beneficial rather than the converse:

> Jack Sprat, could eat no fat;
> His doctor told him not to,
> But as his wife did not like waste,
> She felt that she had got to!
> She scoffed the butter; drank the cream;
> She ate Jack's bacon rind,
> Yet stayed as thin as any rake,
> No matter how she dined!
> At fifty eight Jack passed away,
> His heart could take no more;
> His wife went on her merry way,
> And now she's ninety four!

Overweight people, can also be disciples of Methuselah, as confirmed by the following:

> Old Methuselah, always ate,
> Whatever he found, on his plate,
> And never, as people, now do,
> Did he note, the amount,
> Of the calorie count,
> Even if, there was ample, for two!
> He wasn't concerned, when at dinner, he sat,
> Devouring a roast, or a pie,
> That it might, in fact, be loaded with fat,
> Or a couple, of vitamins shy!

> He cheerfully chewed, each morsel of food,
> Without, any worries, or fears,
> And though his girth, did grow, and grow,
> He still did live, as you, do know,
> For well over 900 years!

You could then follow on, by saying that an **adverse** spin off from food consumption, is that which occurred, at a recent social, when:

> I sat next to the duchess, at tea;
> It was just as I feared it would be!
> Her rumblings abdominal
> Were truly phenomenal,
> But everyone thought it was me!

She couldn't remember her rumba

Although many folk in their nineties are still **physically** mobile, their memories will have certainly begun to fade, as was the case for Mabel in the following dotty ditty, who, with husband Fred, had entered a senior citizens' dance competition:

> The night before they took to the floor
> To practise their steps and moves and more.
> She was very sexy when doing the jive,
> With wiggling hips and cute duck and dive,
> But she couldn't remember her rumba!
>
> Mabel's foxtrot was certainly quite neat,
> But found Fred a problem with his two left feet!
> So the strain of dancing without any error
> Left dear old Mabel riddled with terror;
> And she couldn't remember her rumba!
>
> The night of the dance Fred was still in a slumber,
> But Mabel turned heads with her sexy number,
> Fred was quite tense and looked rather glum,
> But Mabel drew smiles when she wiggled her bum!
> Though she couldn't remember her rumba!
>
> When time for that came she felt in dead lumber,
> As Fred just stood there like a cu-cumber!
> Soon they got started but were given no score,
> As they got in a tangle and fell on the floor!
> But then she remembered her rumba!

When the judges asked Mabel if she had been drinking, she replied:

'I love a martini,' said Mabel,
'But I only have two at the most.
The first finds me under the table;
The second, under my host!'

— which wasn't as far fetched as it seemed, as when she got to bed that night with Fred, the following 'Giddy ditty' records what she said:

I ran up the door
And opened the stairs;
I said my pyjamas,
And got into my prayers;
I switched off the bed,
And climbed into the light;
All because you kissed me – earlier tonight!

Greetings card verses

Sadly, there are times in life, when some folk, would dearly love to send someone a 'backhanded' greetings card, but are thwarted in that respect due to the fact that they can't be found in the shops! Hence, for those so inclined, the following selection could well be fitted in to blank cards, though primarily, they are intended to be chuckle-raisers within appropriate social environments:

To neighbours from Hell, who are finally moving house, the message could read:

> Gone, you are, but not forgotten,
> Holy cow! You were quite rotten!
> Rowdy parties, full of yobs,
> Your car on bricks, just like the slobs.
> But we're not bitter; no indeed,
> Though through your letterbox we've pee'd!
> And worse for you, there's something grimmer;
> We have still got your garden strimmer!

On the first wedding anniversary following an acrimonious divorce, this might be apt:

> This little card is just to say
> That we were married on this day,
> But wish I'd known before we wed,
> That you'd be like a corpse in bed!

To a colleague, on her most unexpected(?) promotion:

> As good wishes go, we send you an ocean;
> You've really earned your new promotion!
> You're attractive, bubbly (if not too bright!),

> You've worked your pants off every night!
> But oh, we're laughing till we sob;
> You bonked the boss to get the job!

And where such boss-bonking has resulted in a far from pretty baby being born, the 'congratulations' card could read:

> Be proud of baby; nay, don't weep;
> Remember looks are but skin deep.
> Thick 'wire wool' locks and gargoyle face,
> Can hide an angel, full of Grace;
> And as she grows do not despair,
> She may well lose that facial hair!
> And rest assured, when she's earning.
> She'll make a fortune out of gurning!

Try it the other way round

Going back more than a few years to the days of radio comedy, it is nice to be able to recall the humour of a marvellous Lancashire comedian called Al Read, who didn't tell jokes per se, but instead had the knack of generating laughter through alerting audiences to the funny side of everyday human situations, such as in the following dotty ditty, which centres round the situation that unfolds when Al's next door neighbour seeks his help with a problem:

> Upstairs on his landing, where both of us flew,
> Was his wardrobe jammed tight in the door.
> Well, we pushed it and shoved it, but all we could do
> Was to wedge the thing more than before!
>
> We hammered the doors off and pulled out the drawers,
> But it wouldn't go anywhere near,
> Then at midnight we heard a 'rat tat' and a pause,
> And a voice shouted: 'What's all this 'ere?'
>
> It was Constable Bright, who said: 'What's all this din?'
> He said: 'Come on; it's not very nice!'
> Then he took in the scene; tucked in his chin,
> And said: 'Now listen; take my advice.'
>
> He said: 'Try it the other way round.'
> He said: 'Try it, but don't make a sound;
> If I hear one squeak – if you so much as speak –
> I shall have you inside for the rest of the week!'
>
> As it lifted, it jarred on the paintwork,
> Rasped out as clear as could be.
> He said: 'Caught yer', and laughed; I said: 'Don't be so daft;
> It's those onions I had for my tea!'

I said: 'Try it the other way round;
There's a way, and it's got to be found.'
Said the copper: 'That's true… push 'ard, and you too;
And I'll whip out me truncheon and lever it through.'

Well the wardrobe went in like a charmer,
Said my neighbour: 'It's in, there's no doubt;
We could put up a flag, but there's only one snag,
I've been struggling to get the thing out!'

The constable got on his bike in disgust,
And by taking the wardrobe apart,
The two of us pushed and we shoved and we just
Got it wedged like it was at the start!

It was dawn when the man from next door made a call,
'This brickwork's too flimsy,' he said,
'And by banging that wardrobe so hard on the wall,
You keep knocking my wife out of bed!'

He said: 'Try it the other way round,
There's a theory I'd like to propound,
If we all get inside, with the weight it might slide,
And I think you might find you'll get quite a nice ride!'

'Oh, I can't live with this,' said the neighbour,
'It's a fact I'd be willing to prove.'
He said: 'Is it wedged tight?' I said: 'Yes.' He said: 'Right!'
'Let's leave it; I'll bloody well move!'

If you can emulate a northern accent when delivering that item, it will further improve the impact on the audience.

Talking of policemen, and providing your audience is broad-minded, then you can generate a little mirth by stating that recently, a class of six-year-olds certainly saw police folk in a different light when their teacher asked them to compile short ditties using the word 'pistol' correctly. Young Fred duly came up with:

My father is a policeman;
And wears a suit of blue.
He always carries a truncheon,
And often, a pistol, too.

'Ten out of ten!' said the teacher.

Then little Johnny recited:

My father's not a policeman,
And wears no suit of blue.
He collects the dole at 12 o'clock,
And is on the piss till two!

The boy stood on the burning deck

When writing her poem 'Casabianca', the short-lived poet Felicia Dorothea Hemans (1793-1835) could never have imagined how much her immortal line 'The boy stood on the burning deck' would later be exploited by humorists and satirists. Thus, for the sake of completeness, a small sample of such ditties now follows:

> The boy stood on the burning deck,
> On the burning deck stood he.
> If it wasn't for the burning deck,
> He'd be in the ruddy sea!

> The boy stood on the burning deck,
> His feet all covered in blisters;
> He'd burnt the seat of his trousers out,
> So he had to wear his sister's!

Now one that's a little earthy:

> The boy stood on the burning deck,
> Picking his nose like mad;
> He rolled the bits in little balls
> And flicked them at his dad!

And one a little risqué:

> The boy stood on the burning deck,
> Playing a game of cricket;
> The ball went up his trouser le,
> And hit his middle wicket!

Finally, a totally unconnected ditty to catch folk out who are prone to jump in a little too quickly:

> Simple Simon met a pie-man
> Going to the fair.
> Said Simple Simon to the pie-man:
> 'Pray **what** have you got there?
> Said the pie-man to Simple Simon:
> **'Pies – you fool!'**

A ditty not to be sniffed at!

As a sequel to 'Pete the piddling pup', and providing your audience is not averse to items which are perhaps a little earthy but tastefully put together, this item could be an unusual follow up:

> The dogs they held a meeting,
> They came from near and far;
> Some in little aeroplanes,
> And some by motor car!
>
> Before they reached the meeting place,
> Instructions they all took.
> They had to take their buttocks off
> And hang them on a hook!
>
> Then in single file they entered,
> Every mother, son and sire,
> But ere the meeting had begun,
> A big dog shouted, 'Fire!'
>
> Out they dashed in panic,
> Not having time to look,
> And grabbed the nearest buttocks
> From off the nearest hook.
>
> But when they put their buttocks on,
> They soon felt rather sore,
> Because the dogs had buttocks,
> That they'd never had before!
>
> And that is why you see today
> A dog will leave his bone,
> To sniff a new dog's buttocks,
> As he's looking for his own!

Una's ode

Having come to the end of the 'Dotty Ditty' section, it is certainly pertinent to remember that another ingredient of laughter is that it is **infectious**, in the sense that it impels those within earshot of it to get in laughter mood **themselves**! Not only that; it can also inspire some folk to come up with creations of their **own**, which was in fact the case with a lady called Una (not Una Stubbs; but just as lovely!), who I met during a cruise.

Seeing me on deck on sea days, forever writing odes and ditties, humorous banter began to pass between us, which ultimately inspired Una to compile a saucy song with the title 'Down Below', of which my rather corrupted version has already been featured within this compendium's 'Saucy Songs' section!

So why am I telling you all this? Simply to alert you to the fact, that if **you** find that **you also** have a bent for compiling verse, whether droll or serious, then you can be sure that developing that ability **will** be very satisfying and long lasting, and will also enable you to give much pleasure to the many folk with whom you socialise through the years. So why not start experimenting now, as you **could** discover that you have a latent talent just waiting to be tapped!

That was, and is, certainly the case with Una, who in further exemplification of the point just made, also came up with a tribute to yours truly, of which a modestly revised version now follows:

Arthur's a chap, from Leamington Spa,
Who writes droll ditties and will go far...
...across, the oceans he'll sail away,
Regaling passengers every day.

While in Madeira, supping the wine,
His witty ditties will go down fine.
Then back to the ship he will walk tall,
As due to him they'll have all had a ball!

In Rio town, where the beat is hot,
He will find himself a thrilling spot
On Sugar Loaf Mountain's lofty height;
Then 'Down below' he will, recite!

Back at sea and with winds still fair,
King Neptune will be waiting there,
To beckon Arthur around the Horn,
And greet him as to the manor born!

But back once more in calypso land,
He'll mingle with the folk on hand,
Making notes and collecting data
For next performance on board later!

Funny happ'nings are what he's penned,
Ditties and odes seem never to end,
If all could see that having some fun
Make **lots** quite happy; not just **one**!

This simple ode you might think naff,
I'm only trying to raise a laugh,
Like you do, Arthur – but please don't fret;
You've got no competition – yet!

As you are now about to leave the Dotty Ditties, and move on the Monologue Mirth, herewith a blessing to send you on your way:

May there always be work for your hands to do;
May your purse always hold, a coin or two;
May the sun always shine on your window pane;
May a rainbow be certain to follow each rain;
May the hand of a friend always be near you;
May God fill your heart with gladness to cheer you!

Monologue Mirth

Within this section, you will find a miscellany of letters, articles, prayers, and other solo recitals, all of which differ from the contents of the 'Saucy Song' and 'Dotty Ditty' sections, by virtue of the total absence of any poetic rhyming. Again, many have found favour with a variety of audiences, so whether you are a speechmaker, socialite or an entertainer in some other form, I feel sure that you will find something you can use within the following collection.

So where do we begin? Well, as within most social gatherings there is nearly always someone well known for his capacity for drink, you can ensure that the laugh will be on him by telling the company that his wife has given you a copy of a letter he recently received from the local vicar, and you thought they would find its contents interesting:

Rev. Abraham Blythe's letter

Dear Mr (insert name as appropriate),

Although you will have doubtless heard of my nationwide campaign in the cause of temperance, you may nevertheless be unaware that during the past 14 years, I have made an annual tour of Scotland and the north of England, including Manchester, Liverpool, Glasgow, and Birmingham, to deliver a series of lectures on the evils of drinking!

During those tours, I was always accompanied by a young friend and assistant – David Powell – as, despite his excellent background, he was a pathetic example of a young life completely ruined by excessive indulgence in whisky and women!

David would appear with me at each lecture and sit on the platform, wheezing and staring at the audience through bleary, bloodshot eyes, sweating profusely, picking his nose, passing wind, and making obscene gestures; while I would point him out as a tragic example of what drinking etc can do to a young person!

Last month, David unfortunately (but not surprisingly!) died, and as a mutual friend gave me your name, I wondered if you would care to take David's place on my next tour?

Trusting this finds you in good spirits in more ways than one!
Yours in faith,

Rev. Abraham Blythe, D.D.

Inland Revenue letter

As a result of having received, what he considered to be a grossly unfair tax demand, an infuriated, low paid wage earner called Mr Addison wrote a vitriolic letter to the Inland Revenue, which its Customer Relations Manager, Mr H.J.Lee, responded to with such subtlety that his letter was ultimately featured in the Guardian newspaper; an edited version of which is as follows:

Dear Mr Addison,

I am writing to express our thanks for your more than prompt reply to our latest communication, and also to answer the points you raised. As ever, I shall address them in the order in which they occurred.

Firstly then, I must take issue with your description of that communication as a **'begging letter'***, as it should be more properly referred to as a* **'tax demand'***. This is how we at the Inland Revenue have always, for reasons of accuracy, referred to such documents!*

Secondly, your frustration resulting from us adding (as you say) to the 'endless stream of crapulent, whining, and panhandling, vomiting daily through your letterbox on to the doormat' has been noted. However, whilst I have naturally never seen the other letters to which you refer, I would cautiously suggest, that if they **are** *from 'pauper councils, Lombardy pirate banking houses, and pissant gas-mongerers', then your decision to 'file them next to the toilet, in case of emergencies', is at best ill advised, as in common with my own organisation, it is unlikely that any of the senders of those letters see you as a 'lackwit bumpkin', or come to that, even as a 'sodding charity', as you put it! It is far more likely that they see you as a British citizen with a responsibility to contribute to the upkeep of the nation as a whole.*

Thirdly, whilst there may be a **grain** *of truth in your assertion that the taxes you pay 'go to shore up the canker-blighted, toppling folly that is the Public Services', a moment's rudimentary calculation ought to rid you of the notion that the government expects you in any way to 'stump up for the* **whole** *damned party'* **yourself!** *The estimates you provide for the*

Chancellor's disbursement of the funds levied by taxation, whilst colourful, are a little wide of the mark, as **less** *than you seem to imagine, is spent on 'junkets for Bunterish lickspittles and dancing whores'; whilst* **far more** *than you have accounted for is allocated to 'that box-ticking façade of a university system', as you put it.*

And now a couple of technical points arising from your direct queries:

Firstly, the reason we don't simply address you as 'Muggins' on the envelope is due to the vagaries of the postal system, and secondly, you can rest assured that 'sucking the very marrows of those with nothing else to give' has never been considered by us as practical, as even if the existence of the Personal Allowance didn't render that irrelevant, the sheer medical logistics involved in marrow sucking would make that financially unviable!

Hence, I do hope that this has helped to clear the air, and without wishing to influence your decision in any way, must mention that should you ultimately decide to 'give the whole foul jamboree up, and go and live in India', you would still owe us the money. So please send it to us by Friday.

Yours sincerely,

H.J.Lee
Customer Relations

Certainly a lovely example of how humour can even emerge from the most vitriolic language, as well as an excellent lesson in using an irate individual's own dialogue to respond to him without fuelling further provocation!

Letter to the Leith Police

In these days where standards of service, as well as behaviour, are deteriorating more and more, even the Police Service is not exempt from such failings, as the following version of **e-mail** correspondence, between a frustrated Edinburgh citizen, and the Leith Police, duly confirms:

Dear Sir/ Madam/ automated telephone answering service,

Having spent the last twenty minutes waiting for someone at the Leith Police Station to pick up the phone, I have decided to abandon that idea, and try e-mailing you instead. Perhaps you would **now** be so kind, as to pass this message on to your Station colleagues – by means of smoke signal, carrier pigeon, or Ouija Board!

Whilst I am writing this e-mail, there are 11 failed medical experiments [which you probably call, youths!], in West Cromwell Street, which is just off Commercial Street, in Leith. Six of them, seem happy enough playing a game, that involves kicking a football against an iron gate, with the force of a meteorite. This causes an earth shattering CLANG, which echoes throughout the entire building. The game is now in its third week, and as I'm unsure how the scoring system works, I haven't a clue, when it will **damn well** finish!

The remaining five walking abortions, are happily rummaging through several bags of rubbish, and items of furniture, that someone has so thoughtfully dumped beside the wheelie bins. One of them has found a saw, and is setting about a discarded chair, like a beaver on speed! I fear that it is only a matter of time, before they turn their limited talents to the bottle of calor gas that is lying on its side, between the two bins! If they could be relied upon, to only blow their own arms and legs off, I would happily leave them to it, and even go so far as to lend them the matches! Unfortunately, they are far more likely to blow up half the street as well, and I've just finished decorating the kitchen!

What I suggest, is that rather than replying to this e-mail with worthless assurances that the matter is now being looked into, and will shortly be dealt with, why not leave it until the **one** night of the year (probably bath night!), when there are no mutants around, and then drive up the street in a panda car, before doing a three point turn, and disappearing again? This will of course serve no other purpose, than to remind us what policemen actually look like!

I trust that when I take a claw hammer to the skull of one of these throwbacks, you'll do me the same courtesy of giving me a four month head start, before coming to arrest me.

I remain sir, your obedient servant,

Hamish McSweeney

* * *

Dear Mr McSweeney,

I have read your e-mail, and understand your frustration over the problems caused by the youths playing in your area, and, the problems you have encountered, in trying to contact the Police.

As the Community Beat Officer for your street, I should therefore like to extend an offer of discussing the matter fully with you.

Should you wish to discuss the matter further, then please provide contact details [i.e. address/telephone number], and also when that may be suitable for you.

Regards.

P.C. Plod
Community Beat Officer

* * *

Dear P.C. Plod,

First of all, I should like to thank you for your speedy response to my original e-mail. Sixteen hours and thirty eight minutes, must be a personal record for the Leith Police, and so you may rest assured, that I will forward that data to Norris McWhirter, for inclusion in his next edition, of the Guinness Book of Records!

Secondly, I was delighted to hear that our street has its own Community Beat Officer. May I be the first to congratulate you on your <u>co</u>vert skills, as in the five years that I have lived in West Cromwell Street, I have never even seen you, let alone spoken to you! Do you hide up a tree, or have you gone deep undercover, and actually infiltrated the gang itself? Are you the one with the acne, and the moustache on his forehead, or the one with the chin like a wash basin? It's surely only a question of time before you are headhunted by MI5!

Whilst I realise, that there may be far more serious crimes taking place in Leith, such as smoking in public places, or being Muslim without due care and attention, is it too much to ask, for a policeman to explain to these twats [in words of no more than two syllables], that it might be better for them to play their strange football game elsewhere. The pitch behind the Citadel, or the one at DKs, are both still within spitting distance, as is the bottom of Leith Dock!

Should you wish to discuss these matters further, please feel free to call me on Edinburgh 666. If, after 25 minutes, I have still failed to answer, I'll buy you a large one, in the Compass Bar.

Regards

Hamish McSweeney

P.S. If you think that this is sarcasm, think yourself lucky that you don't work for the Cleansing Department!

Seamus O'Boyle's letter to his doctor

Changing tack, the following letter is an amusing example of innocent Irish naivety, which, like the Irish flavoured offerings within the 'Dotty Ditty' section, could be used to advantage at St. Patrick's Day parties, as well as other social occasions:

Dr. Michael Maloney,
St. Patrick's General Hospital,
Ballybunnion,
Co. Kerry

Dear Dr Maloney,

Please don't think this a load of baloney, Dr Maloney, but for more reasons than I care to mention, I wish to apply for an operation to make me sterile!

Why, bejabbers? Well, doctor, one thing I **can** *tell you is that as I've already got* **seven children**, *after only* **seven years** *of marriage, I've come to the conclusion that contraceptives are totally useless – honest to God!*

In fact, I'm thinking of suing the chemist who sold me a sheath, as although I couldn't see how stretching a Durex over his thumb could prevent babbies, I bought it in good faith, but Bridie still got pregnant!

We were then advised to try the coil, but no matter which way we screwed, we still couldn't get the thing to fit!

Although the Dutch cap gave us new hope, and didn't affect our sex life, it still gave Bridie headaches – as despite buying the largest size available, it was much too tight across her forehead!

Finally, we tried the pill, but as it kept falling out, Bridie put it between her knees, which **did** *stop me reaching the 'danger zone', to be sure – but only until the night she forgot the wretched thing, and as sure as God made little apples, she got pregnant again!*

But we didn't give up, and after three 'Hail Maries', we remembered that Father O'Casey once suggested we should try the 'rhythm' method.

But after doing the tango and the samba, and nearly rupturing myself in the cha cha cha, Bridie still got pregnant – and it wasn't easy getting a dance band, at two o'clock in the morning, either!

So in desperation, Bridie phoned her friend, Soairsie O'Toole, who suggested that if we made love while breast feeding, we should be alright – but although it wasn't a patch on Guinness, and I did finish up with a clear skin and silky hair, the wife was still pregnant, begorra!

Although we did consider the 'old wives' remedy' of getting Bridie to jump up and down **after** *intercourse, we realised that if she was to do that, after all the breast feeding, she'd end up with two black eyes and as like as not, she'd knock herself out!*

So the only remedy left to us was to use the safe period, but as we were then living with the in-laws, we had to wait three weeks before we had the house to ourselves, and that didn't work either!

So, Dr Maloney, you've just **got to** *give me the operation, and if that doesn't work, bejabbers, Bridie and I have agreed to revert to* **oral** *sex, though just* **talking** *about it will be a far cry from the real thing, honest to God!*

Yours in faith,

Seamus O'Boyle

P.S. The other side of the coin, doctor, is, that if we have another babby, the kids with have to sleep four in a bed, and as three are already bed wetters, the shallow end is going to be overcrowded – and even if we got another £16 per week of family benefit, we still couldn't afford to move to a bigger house!

As ever with items of an Irish flavour, audience impact will be further enhanced if you can manage to recite that letter with an Irish accent!

As Bridie and Seamus certainly appeared to enjoy the pleasures of the night, it would be no surprise if Seamus's view of kissing was epitomised by the following words:

Some kisses take only two seconds,
They're gentle and go on the cheeks,
But I like the ones you plant on the lips,
And can last for two or three weeks!

Moreover, if Bridie had had to write a message for the local newspaper Anniversary Column, it is likely that the narrative wouldn't be much different from one that I believe originally emanated from the Yorkshire Evening Post some years ago, which read:

To Fred, on our 17th Wedding Anniversary:

When I'm sad and dreary,
And think all hope has gone;
When I'm tired and weary,
I think of you with **nothing on**!

Lots of love, as usual,
Mabel xxx

Paddy's letter to his Bank Manager

As a parody of an actual letter written in the 1920s, and in further confirmation of the uniquely quaint use of the English language by the Irish, look no farther than the following letter from an exasperated Paddy O'Callaghan to his bank manager, who has requested an explanation as to why Paddy has not reduced his overdraft. For best results when reciting it to an audience, not only do you need to endeavour to do so with an Irish accent, but you should also deliver the various category group lists in a rapid, machine gun-like manner:

Dear Mr Mannering!

The reason I have been unable to reduce my overdraft is simply that I have been held up; held down; bagged; walked on; sat upon; flattened out; and squeezed by income tax; council tax; car tax; corporation tax; gains tax; and then by every society and organisation that the inventive mind of man has conceived (in order to extract what I may have, or may not have, in my possession), including famine relief; flood relief; and **comic relief**; *red cross: black cross;* **double cross**; *and every hospice in this town and country!*

The government has so controlled my business that I now don't really know who owns it!

I'm **ins**pected; **sus**pected; *examined; re-examined; informed; required; and commanded; so much that I don't know who I am; where I am; or why I am here at all!*

All **I am** *aware of is that I am supposed to be an inexhaustible source of money for every known need, desire or hope of the human race!*

Because I will not sell all I have, and go out and beg, borrow, and steal money to give away, I am cussed; **dis**cussed; *boycotted; talked to; talked about; lied to; lied about; held up; hung up; robbed; and ruined!*

The only reason why I am clinging on to life now is to see what the Hell happens next!

But I will be in on Monday to reduce my overdraft, as I've just received a **tax rebate***!*

Yours (still) **faith***fully,*

Paddy O'Callaghan

Barnacle Bill with a difference

Although much of what we read in the national press tends to be bereft of humour and happiness, fortunately, there are exceptions, as exemplified by the singular plight of the British holidaymaker in the amended version of an article from 'The People' dated 2nd October, 2005, which now follows:

'Having dozed off while **nude** sun bathing at a Fijian beach resort, a British tourist was suddenly awakened by the wash of the incoming tide, and to his surprise and embarrassment, he discovered that a **barnacle** had attached itself to his todger!

The embarrassment proved even more acute, as on arrival at the hospital, the arousal generated by the presence of a very attractive, nubile young nurse merely caused the barnacle to gain an even tighter grip on the Briton's expanding member!

To his relief (!), a **male** nurse was summoned, who eventually succeeded in prizing the barnacle off, thereby allowing everything to return to normal – not least the 'todger'!

Fortunately for the Briton, he had arranged travel insurance with a major company called 'Europe assistance', and ultimately received £50, towards pain relief for his ordeal!

Later liaison with those insurers revealed that they often handle unusual claims, a recent example of which involved a tourist in Cyprus who accidentally slapped **Superglue** on his backside, after mistaking it for **haemorrhoid cream**! The subsequent operation to free his bowels was a relief, in more ways than one, and also resulted in a successful claim for £800 to cover medical expenses!'

It would come as no surprise if the resultant publicity ultimately led our Fiji sun worshipper to acquire the nickname 'Barnacle Bill' – especially, if his Christian name was in fact William!'

As stated in the preamble to this section, these letters and articles etc are ideal items to have handy at dinners, parties and other such functions, where there would be opportunities to recite items in monologue fashion.

Whiff of fear

More recently, an article from the December 7th 2006 issue of the Daily Mirror featured a situation that I sense could only happen in America! The amended version of that article will thus now make everything clear:

> Although it is not uncommon for an airliner to be grounded due to severe **exterior** turbulence, an American Airways scheduled flight from Washington D.C. to Dallas was actually forced to make an emergency landing due to severe **interior** turbulence, caused by the continuous breaking of wind by one of the female passengers!
>
> Being acutely embarrassed by the awful smell which her continuous flatulence was generating, the unfortunate lady endeavoured to quell the stench by burning it away with lighted matches!
>
> Not surprisingly, the smell of burning caused some of the 96 passengers on board to raise the alarm, and on landing all were taken off and searched for **explosives**!
>
> When interrogated, the unfortunate woman admitted that as a medical condition made her break wind almost continuously; and as she didn't want to 'gas' her fellow passengers, she had been driven to lighting matches in the hope of burning it all off!
>
> When telling reporters that the woman had now been permanently banned from American Airline flights, the airline spokesman went on to state, that there would be no '**trumped up**' charges!
>
> As news of it spread across America, the occurrence duly prompted local press headlines, such as:
>
> '**Whiff of fear** on American Airlines jet!'
>
> and

'American Airlines jet compelled to make a **bum**py landing!'

This is yet another example of the inescapable human habit that serves to further justify the in-depth analysis thereof, to be found in the Epilogue later in this book.

Life before the language of computers

When there is talk of how things have changed over the years, or the audience is of mature age, the following offering will strike a few chords as well as generating a chuckle, especially on delivery of the punch line:

Memory was something which faded with age!
An **application** was usually for a job!
A **programme** related to TV or radio!
A **cursor** was someone who was always swearing!
A **keyboard** was on a piano!
A **web** was a spider's home!
A **virus** was the flu!
A **CD** was a cash deposit!
A **hard drive** was a trip along the M25 at rush hour!
A **mouse pad** was where a mouse lived!
And if you had a **3½ inch floppy**, you certainly didn't tell anyone about it!
It's a crazy world!

Whatever befalls us

When someone is bleating about his bad luck, or you are in the company of folk of mature age, then the following brief monologue will again strike several chords, as well as a chuckle on hitting the punch line. Just get into it by saying:

When an octogenarian I know called Fred heard a young chap at the club bemoaning his bad luck, Fred couldn't help saying:

'If you think you're unlucky; what about me? I've had two heart bypass operations; a hip replacement; two new knee joints; I'm half blind and am currently fighting prostate cancer and diabetes; I take 14 different medications every day, which leave me dizzy, winded, and subject to blackouts; my circulation is poor, with hardly any feeling in my hands and feet; I have bouts of dementia; and I can't remember whether I'm 78, or 87– but I still count myself lucky, as I have still got my Driving Licence!'

Sometimes bad luck is **self-inflicted**, as confirmed by the following Dotty Ditty:

Doctor Bell, fell down the well,
And broke his collar bone.
A doctor, should attend the sick,
And leave the well alone!

A snake called Pete

As a sequel to 'Pete the piddling **pup**', to be found in the 'Dotty Ditty' section, the following monologue, involving a **snake** called Pete, should get a good audience response, in view of its tongue-twisting nature and its veiled link to toilet activity:

Pete was a little snake, who lived in a snake pit with his mother.
One day, Pete was **hissing** in the pit, when his mother said, 'Pete, if you must **hiss** in the pit, go outside the pit, and **hiss**'.
So Pete went outside the pit to **hiss**!
Pete was **hissing** around, and then leaned over, and **hissed** in the pit once again. Pete's mother heard Pete **hissing** in the pit, and said:
'Pete, if you must **hiss** in a pit, go over to Mrs Potts' pit, and **hiss** in her pit!'
Pete duly went over to Mrs Potts' pit to **hiss**
Mrs Potts was not at home – but he **hissed** in her pit anyway!
While Pete was **hissing** in Mrs Potts' pit, Mrs Potts came home and found Pete **hissing** in her pit, and said:
'Pete, if you must **hiss** in a pit, don't **hiss** in my pit! Go home to your own pit, and **hiss**!
This made Pete very sad, and he cried all the way home!
When Pete got home, his mother found him crying, and said: 'Pete, what is the matter?'
Pete said: 'I went over to Mrs Potts' pit to **hiss**, but Mrs Potts was not at home, so I **hissed** in her pit anyway!
Then Mrs Potts came home, and found me **hissing** in her pit, and said: 'Pete, if you must **hiss** in a pit, go home and **hiss** in your own pit'.
This made Pete's mother very angry, and she said: 'That mean old lady! I knew Mrs Potts when she didn't even have a pit to **hiss** in!'

The faster you can recite this monologue, without falling into the trap of spoonerising **hiss** and **pit**, the more impressive your delivery will be; but equally, should you trip over your tongue and the wrong word does come out, the audience will certainly have a chuckle, despite the earthy nature of that dialogue!

Life in the new millennium

When folk are talking of how **well off** we all are now the new millennium has arrived, you can strike a fair few chords within any gathering by paradoxically drawing attention to the many **adverse** 'side affects' that the improved living conditions have produced, as summarised by the following comparisons, which ultimately lead to the concluding good advice:

> We **spend more**
> And **enjoy less;**
> We have **bigger houses**
> But **smaller families;**
> We make **more compromises**
> But have **less time;**
> We have **more knowledge**
> But **less judgement;**
> We have **more medicines**
> But **poorer health;**
> We have **increased** our **possessions**
> But **reduced** our **values;**
> We have **conquered outer space**
> But **not our inner space;**
> We have **higher income**
> But **lower morals;**
> We have **more freedom**
> But **less joy;**
> We have **more food**
> But **less nutrition;**
> We have **finer houses**
> But **more broken homes.**
>
> And that's not all!

We also talk much, love little and hate too much!

We've been to the moon and back - but find it hard to cross the road, and meet our neighbour!

Two incomes are needed for a house purchase – but divorces are increasing!

Life should be a series of moments of enjoyment – not just a survival course!

So don't keep anything for a special occasion – treat every day lived as a special occasion!

Spend more time with friends and family.

And savour the view of this wonderful world without dwelling on your needs.

Although not a humorous monologue per se, it is certainly something that will get the audience thinking, and is an ideal prelude to the 'Company statistics' item that follows on from this offering.

Company statistics

There is one sphere of human activity that never escapes the attention of the humorist, and to lead you (or your audience) to it, the following questions must first be asked. In order for you to give the answers some thought, before the are revealed, they have been relegated to the next page:

(i) Can you imagine working for a company or firm that has over 500 employees, of whom:

29 have been accused of spouse abuse;
7 have been arrested for fraud;
19 have been accused of writing bad cheques;
117 have either directly, or indirectly, bankrupted at least two businesses;
3 have served time for assault;
71 cannot obtain a credit card, due to an inadequate credit rating;
14 have been arrested on drug-related charges;
8 have been arrested for shoplifting;
21 were, at the time of compiling this item (2006), defendants in law suits;
84 had been arrested for drink-driving the year previous to this listing (2005)?

(ii) Can you guess which well known 'firm' the foregoing actually relates to?

For the answers, see below.

Company statistics – Answers to (i) & (ii)

As you may well have already guessed, the answer could only be:

The 535 Members of the houses of Parliament, i.e. the same 'firm' that cranks out dozens of new laws each year, designed to keep **the rest of us** in line!

As I said at the outset, governments are a prime target for the humorist, and ours is no exception. But in this particular instance, any funny side has really been drowned by the dreadful picture it portrays, of such a significant segment of our leaders!

Asylum

As there is no perfect government, the British Government is no exception, and one aspect which the **indigenous population** has understandably, been very concerned about during the last decade is how easy it apparently is for asylum-seekers not only to become citizens of the U.K., but also to obtain generous benefits and allowances – so much so that in eastern Europe, Britain **really has** actually been given the nickname: 'Treasure Island'!

As ever, this has not escaped the attention of the humorist, and thus if you utilise the foregoing paragraph to introduce the following monologue, it should certainly strike plenty of chords, and evoke wry smiles, if not chuckles:

In the U.K., the TV programme everyone wants to get on is Channel 4's 'Deal or no deal', but the TV programme that has really caught on in Eastern Europe and Asia is one called **'Asylum'**!

Although that programme is naturally transmitted in the languages of the various countries involved, I have actually managed to obtain an English translation of last Tuesday's narrative, which I feel you will find most enlightening. It thus reads as follows:

We welcome new viewers to today's programme with the news that this is **another opportunity** to take part in our ongoing competition called **hijack an airliner and win a council house**!

We have already given away millions of pounds and hundreds of dream homes, due to the generosity of our sponsor – the British taxpayer!

Understandably, it is the fastest growing game on this planet, due to the fact that:

(a) providing you **don't** hold a **valid** British passport, **anyone** can play; and

(b) you only need to know **one word** in English, which is **asylum!**

Prizes include:

(i) All expenses paid accommodation.
(ii) Cash benefits of a minimum of £180 per week.
(iii) The opportunity to increase earnings even further, through begging; mugging, or accosting motorists at traffic lights!

The competition is open to anyone buying a ticket, or stowing away on one of our agent's airlines, ferries or Eurostar, and in preparation for this, all you need to do, is to destroy all your personal I.D. documents, and remember the magic password: **Asylum** !

Only last week, 140 Taliban viewers were flown 'goat class' from Kabul to our international reception centre at Stansted, where the local law enforcement officers were on hand to fast track them to their luxury £200 per night accommodation, at the four-star Hilton Hotel!

Accordingly, they joined thousands of other lucky winners who are already staying in hotels all over Britain, the most popular destinations being the White Cliffs of Dover, the world famous Toddington Service Station, and the Money Trees in Croydon!

Should any aspect of this competition still be unclear, there is no need to phone a friend or ask the audience, as dozens of solicitors, social workers and councillors are readily on hand to enable you to apply for legal aid!

What is more, don't worry if you are an Afghan dissident, Albanian gangster, Bin Laden activist, Kosovan drugster, Tamil tiger or Somali guerrilla; just get along to the airport, lorry park or ferry terminal and go straight to Britain, where you will be guaranteed to become one of the tens of thousands of lucky winners in what is now the fastest growing game in the world!

Everyone's a winner when they play **Asylum**!

In fairness, it is must be said that many Easterners **do** come to Britain with the **right credentials**; but as ever, the few that don't can give their compatriots an unwarranted bad name, and duly give satirists ammunition for producing monologues such as this.

It is no lark, building an ark

Completing what in a sense has become a trilogy of governmentally influenced monologues, what follows is a skit on how much the 'Big brother' regulatory syndrome is now impinging on so many aspects of life in Britain. By using that message as an introduction, the following offering will certainly strike many chords with your audience:

In 2006, God spoke to Noah, who was living **in England**, and said:

'Once again, the world has become wicked and over-populated, and I see the end of all flesh before me. Therefore, build another ark and save two of every living thing, along with a few **good** humans!'

God then gave Noah, the **CAD** (i.e. Computer Aided Design!) drawings and said:

'You have got six months to build the ark before it will start raining continuously for forty days and forty nights.'

Six months later, God looked down from Heaven, and not only noticed Noah weeping in his back garden, but also, that there was no ark to be seen, which duly caused God to shout out:

'Noah, the rain is about to start, but where is the ark?'

Noah replied: 'Forgive me Lord, but things have changed so much since I built the first one!

Firstly, I discovered that I needed **Building Regulations approval**, because the ark was over 30 metres square!

Then, I've had an ongoing argument with the **Fire Brigade**, who insist that I need a **Sprinkler System**! Now my neighbours are claiming, that I should have obtained **Planning Permission**, prior to building the ark in my garden, because it represented **site development** – even though, in my view, it was a **temporary structure** – and as they are also alleging that its roof is too high, I am currently having to appeal to the **Secretary of State**!

Getting the wood was another problem, as all the decent trees in this area, have **Preservation Orders** on them, and are evidently within a **site of special scientific interest**, established in order to protect the tawny owl! Although I tried to convince the **environmentalists**, that I needed the wood to actually **save** the owls, it was still to no avail!

When I started collecting the animals, in readiness for the ark's completion, **the R.S.P.C.A.** sued me, on the grounds that I was **confining animals, against their will!**

Then not only the **County Council** but also the **Environment Agency** and the **Rivers Authority** ruled that I couldn't build the ark until they had conducted an **environmental impact study** on your proposed flood! On top of that, I am still trying to resolve a dispute with the **Equal Opportunities Commission**, concerning the number of **B.M.E's** (i.e. **B**lack, & **M**inority **E**thnic groups!) that I am compelled to employ within my **construction team**!

Another problem has been the fact that the **Trade Unions** have prevented me using my sons on the job, as I am evidently only allowed to hire **C.S.C.S.** (i.e. **C**onstruction **S**kills **C**ertification **S**cheme!) accredited workers, with ark building experience!

So forgive me, Lord, but at this rate, it is going to take me at least three years to finish the ark!'

Suddenly, the skies cleared; the sun began to shine, and a rainbow stretched across the sky, which caused Noah to look up to the Heavens in wonder and duly ask God: 'Do you mean, that you are **not** going to destroy this country?'

To which God replied: 'No – the government has already beaten me to it!'

Jack Jones' job specification

As a follow up to 'It is no lark building an ark', you could say that when your friend Jack applied to join Noah's construction team, his Job Spec read as follows:

> My first job was in an **orange juice** factory, but I got **canned** and couldn't **concentrate**!
>
> After that, I tried **tailoring**, but **felt** I wasn't **suited** for it; and as a **baker**, I couldn't make enough **dough**!
>
> Then I thought I'd train to be a **chef**, thinking it would add a bit of **spice** to my life, but I just couldn't find the **thyme**! Next, I worked in a **muffler** factory but soon got **choked off**!
>
> I did manage to get a job in **swimming pool maintenance**, but found it too **draining**!
>
> Then I got work in a **delicatessen**, but I found I couldn't **cut the mustard**!
>
> I also worked as **a lumberjack** in a wood, but they soon gave me the **axe**!
>
> When I tried working in a **shoe factory**, I found that I couldn't **fit in**!
>
> And when I worked in a **gym**, they told me I wasn't **fit** for the job!
>
> Eventually I got a job as an **historian**, but soon realised, that there wasn't any **future** in it!

After studying to become a **doctor**, I found that I didn't have any **patience**!

My best job was as a **musician**, but it really wasn't **note**worthy!

As a professional **fisherman**, I found that I couldn't live, on my **net** income!

My last job was at **Starbuck's**, but I soon had to leave as it was the same old **grind**!

So they call me the **Jack** of all trades – and now I'm retired, I really **am** a Master-**of none**!

So no wonder Noah didn't take him on!

Quirks of the English language

Following the word punning contained in the 'Jack Jones' job specification monologue, you could now add emphasis to the anomalies within the English language by mentioning that you often wonder why:

There's no **ham** in **ham**burger;
Neither **pine** nor **apple** in **pineapple**;
French fries do not come, from **France**;
Quicksand takes you down **slowly**;
Boxing **rings** are **square**;
Guinea pigs are neither from **Guinea** nor are **pigs**.
If writers **write**, why don't fingers **fing**?
If a teacher **taught**, why doesn't a preacher **praught**?
If a veget**arian** eats **veg**etables, what does a humanit**arian** eat?
Why do people **recite** a play, yet **play** at a recital?
When I wind up my watch it **starts**, yet when I wind up a story, it **ends**!
Do **infants** enjoy **infancy** as much as **adults** enjoy **adultery**?
Why is a man who **invests** your money called a **broker**?
Why is a **piano** playing a **pianist**, but a **racing** driver not a **racist**?
Why are wise **men** and wise **guys** opposites?
If **horrific** derives from **horrible**, why doesn't **terrific** derive from **terrible**?
If lawyers are **disbarred** and clergymen **defrocked**,
Can electricians be de**lighted**, musicians de**noted**,
Cowboys de**ranged**, models de**posed**,
Tree surgeons de**barked**, and dry cleaners de**pressed**?
Finally, if people from **Poland** are **Poles**, why aren't people from **Holland** called **Holes**?

Up yours!

For a really singular quirk of the English language, can you think of the one two-letter word that has more different interpretations than all the other two-letter words put together?

No? Then it will surprise you to know, that it is: **up**

Yes, it is a bit of a paradox really, because although **up's** link with 'height' makes it right to say, that the sky is **up** there; or that the frog climbed **up** the pole; or that the monkey is **up** the gum tree; why is it then, that when we emerge from sleep, we wake **up** – despite being **flat** on our backs! – and that a solicitor draws **up** a contract whilst the document lies on the desk, and without actually drawing anything!

But that's just the beginning!

People **queue up** for air tickets, despite being on the **ground floor**!
People **bring up** a family, despite living in a **bungalow**!
People **drink up**, despite the drink going **down** the neck of the drinker!
People **store up** wine, despite putting it **down** in the cellar!
People **pick up** a person for a car ride, without actually **lifting** him/her!
People **cough up** money, without having a **cough**!
People **clear up** a mess, despite it being **on the floor**!
People **hurry up**, without **riding a horse**!
People **catch up** without **catching** anything!

But as Jimmy Cricket would say: 'There's more!'

Amazingly, it is correct to say that you are going **up** to London from the Midlands, even though you would be travelling **south**; and when so and so is mischievous, one can say that he is **up** to his old tricks again; and of course, when somebody annoys you – **up yours!**

In fact, we seem to be quite mixed **up** about **up**; which is not all that surprising, as the O.E.D. (Oxford English Dictionary) gives dozens of different usages of **up** – so if you are **up** to it, why not try to build **up** a list of the many ways **up** can be used, and although that should take **up** quite a lot of your time, don't give **up,** as you may wind **up** with even more than the O.E.D.!

As I sense that you will now want me to dry **up**, I'll wrap this monologue **up** by leaving you with a closing thought, which is that as the **individual** letters in **up** have no connection with height, but instead epitomise what most folk do first thing in the morning, and last thing at night, just what are they referring to?

You've guessed haven't you?! **U**(You) **P**(Pee)!

The Sermon

Another feature of the use of English is the significant variety of dialects that one can come across, according to one's location in England; and of those there are few, if any, more quaint than the 'language' of the London Cockney, which is more familiarly known as Cockney rhyming slang. Hence, after 'The Sermon' which follows, I have added a glossary of 43 terms for the benefit of any reader who is not too familiar with such parlance.

This offering could, in fact, be used to advantage as a follow up to 'The Lord's Prayer' (or 'The London bus driver's lament'), featured within the 'Dotty Ditty' section. The monologue is in the form of a sermon, delivered to a large group of Cockney worshippers, and goes as follows:

'I want to tell you a story. A long time ago, in the days of the Israelites, there lived a poor man who had no **trouble and strife**, as she had run off with a **tea leaf** some years before, and he now lived with his eldest **bricks and mortar**, Mary.

Being very short of **bees and honey**, and unable to pay the **Burton on Trent**, he was tempted to go forth into the **Bristol city** and see what he could **half inch**! He would say to Mary, his **bricks and mortar**, that he was just going for a **ball of chalk**, to buy some tobacco for his **cherry ripe**.

He would then put on his **almond rocks, dicky dirt** and **round the houses,** and set orf down the **frog and toad,** until he reached the outskirts of the **Bristol**. People would then stare at him, for his **dicky dirt** was torn; his **how do you do's** were full of holes; and his coat was very **Westminster Abbey.**

He was also somewhat unclean, as he was too poor to purchase any **Cape of Good Hope,** and not only was his **bushel and peck** extremely **two thirty,** but people passed by on the other side to avoid the **pen and ink!** He was truly an ugly man, as his **north and south** drooped; his **mince pies** were watery; and he had a big red **I suppose!**

One day, his **bricks and mortar** gave him some money, saying: 'Here is a **saucepan lid;** go and buy a loaf of **Uncle Fred,** and a pound of **stand at ease**; but don't tarry in the town, and bring me back what is left of the money, because I'm short of underwear, and need a new pair of **early doors,** as my existing ones are full of holes, which leave me in a continual **George Raft!**'

But instead of returning with the **bees and honey** for his **bricks and mortar's early doors**, he made his way to the **rub a dub** for a **tumble down the sink,** where he indulged himself freely on the wine bottle, and became **elephant's trunk and Mozart!** When the landlord of the **rub a dub** called **bird lime**, the man set orf back towards his **cat and mouse**, reeling all over the **frog and toad,** and drunkenly humming a **stewed prune!**

And it came to **Khyber pass** that as he staggered along, he saw a small brown **Richard the third** on the pavement! As he stared at it lying there at his **plates of meat,** he said:

'Oh, small brown **Richard the third,** how lucky I did not step on you'; and he duly picked it up and put it on top of a wall, so that no one could step on it! Then a rich **four by twoish** merchant, who had witnessed the deed, put his hand into his **sky rocket,** took out a **Lady Godiva,** and gave it to the man, saying: 'I saw you pick up that **Richard the third,** and remove it from the pavement, which was a very kindly act, so please take this **Lady Godiva** for your **froth and bubble!'**

And as the man took it, and went on his way, the **Richard the third** flew back to his nest!

When he arrived home, his **bricks and mortar** was sitting by the **Jeremiah,** on her favourite **Lionel Blair,** but on seeing him tottering, she arose angrily, and said: 'Once again you come home **elephant's trunk and Mozart,** and as you will have spent all the **bees and honey** I gave you, I won't now be able to have my new pair of **early doors** – neither can I have wine, as you do!'

But the man said: 'Fear not, here is a **Lady Godiva**, that **I** earn't for a kindly act', and Mary was overjoyed, and said: 'Thank you, father; now I **can** have my pair of **early doors**, and that kindly act verily means that I'll now have more than enough to cover my **bottle and glass**!

Here endeth this morning's lesson!'

If recited at an even pace (and with a London/Cockney accent, if you can), the multiplicity and quaintness of the inherent rhyming slang will come across as quite funny, and like a lot of Irish monologues, the segment of the audience that is not very familiar with the Cockney vocabulary will be led, for a while, down a blind alley, through mistakenly visualising the **Richard the third** as being something that a dog has left on the pavement – as opposed to a little brown **bird**!

Although vicars are well known for delivering sermons, the following vicar became well known, for something totally different:

The vicar

The vicar parked his little car
Right on a yellow line!
'I'm sorry,' said the constable,
'But this will mean a fine!'

'Dear officer, I'll only need
Two minutes, if permitted.'
'The time is immaterial –
A crime has been committed!'

'Oh! Constable, have pity now;
 Has not my pleading stirred you?
 I only am a poor preacher!'
'I know,' he said, 'I've heard you!'

Glossary of the rhyming slang vocabulary

Trouble and strife – Wife
Tea leaf – Thief
Bricks and mortar – Daughter
Bees and honey – Money
Burton on Trent – Rent
Bristol City – City
Half inch – Pinch
Ball of chalk – Walk
Cherry ripe – Pipe
Almond rocks – Socks
Dicky dirt – Shirt
Round the houses – Trousers
Frog and toad – Road
How do you do's? – Shoes
Westminster Abbey – Shabby
Cape of Good Hope – Soap
Bushel and peck – Neck
Two thirty – Dirty
Pen and ink – Stink
North and south – Mouth
Mince pies – Eyes
I suppose – Nose
Saucepan lid – Quid
Uncle Fred – Bread
Stand at ease – Cheese
Early doors – Draws
George Raft – Draft
Rub a dub – Pub
Tumble down the sink – Drink
Elephant's trunk and Mozart – Drunk
Bird lime – Time
Cat and mouse – House
Stewed prune – Tune

Khyber Pass – Pass
Richard the third – Bird
Plates of meat – Feet
Four by twoish – Jewish
Sky rocket – Pocket
Lady Godiva – Fiver
Froth and bubble – Trouble
Jeremiah – Fire
Lionel Blair – Chair
Bottle and glass* – Arse

* Glass should, of course, be pronounced like glarse, in order to rhyme with 'arse'!

The secret of successful public speaking

When making a speech, a novel way of beginning is to tell the audience that you are actually going to let them into the secret of successful public speaking, and continue by saying that all you have to do is:

> **Firstly** – when **promulgating** your esoteric cogitations, and **articulating** superficial, sentimental, and psychological observations, **beware** of platitudinous ponderosity!
>
> **Secondly** – let your extemporaneous decantations, and unpremeditated expiations, have intelligibility, and veracious veracity, without rodomontade, and thrasonical **bombast**!
>
> **Thirdly** – **sedulously avoid** all polysyllabic profundity; pusillanimous vacuity; pestiferous profanity, and similar transgression!
>
> **In short** – keep it simple, brief, and avoid using any big words!

Prayer prior to Speech

An ideal intro to a speech is to indicate that you always like to begin with a prayer, as follows:

Lord, fill my mouth, with worthwhile stuff,
And nudge me, when, I've said enough!

Another droll intro is simply to say:

Speeches are like babies – easy to conceive but hard to deliver!

But I actually prefer **the ABC/XYZ of public speaking**:

ABC: **A**lways **B**e **C**lear……………………..XYZ: **X**-amine **Y**our **Z**ip !!!

Due to the fact that you will already be standing, this momentary focus on your zip's closure will also enable you to make a gesture of relief – in the nicest sense!

I'm now my own grandfather

Just as the English language can be difficult to follow at times, so too are the complexities of family relationships, as exemplified when Paddy and Mick met in a Dublin bar, and Paddy suddenly exclaimed that he was now his own grandfather, which naturally prompted Mick to ask: how come? What follows, then, is Paddy's explanation, which should be recited at an even pace and, if possible, with a hint of an Irish accent for further impact:

Begorra, it is simple really! I married a **widow** who had a **daughter**, and thus she became my **stepdaughter**! Are you with me so far?

Me **father** then fell in love with me **stepdaughter**, and when he married her, he thus became me **son-in-law**, and she of course became me **stepmother**, because she was me **father's wife**! Are you still with me?

She then had a **son**, who was both me **grandchild** and me **brother** at the same time, because **he** was the **son** of me **father**!

Me **wife** was me **grandmother**, because she was my **stepmother's mother**, and I was my **wife's husband** and **grandchild** at the same time!

Since the **husband** of **a person's** grandmother is **that person's** grandfather, I am now my own **grandfather**!

So Mick, it's as clear as the blue Heaven, above – honest to God!

Yet again, an ideal offering for a St.Patrick's Day party.

And of course, no St. Patrick's day party would be quite the same without a good ration of beer and Guinness, for which participants would readily support the toast embodied in the following ditty:

Charlie Mopps

Once upon this earth there was nowt but misery;
All the people had to drink was ginger beer and tea.
Until there came along a man whose name was Charlie Mopps,
Who did invent a long drink, made from malt and hops.
He might have been an archduke, a sultan or a king,
But now we're gathered here, let us his praises sing.
Look at what he's done for us; he's filled our hearts with cheer;
So God bless Charlie Mopps,
The man who gave us beer!

An Italian in Malta

If you are not into earthy humour, then pass this item by, but for those who are, this monologue is yet another example of how the quirks of the English language can be exploited to advantage by the more risqué humorists. Hence, when you have an appropriate audience in terms of their taste in humour, then reciting this with an Italian accent will maximise its impact.

With that said, I'll now let Luigi take up the story:

'One-a day, I went-a to a big hotel in Malta.

In-a the morning, I go down, to eat-a breakfast, and tell-a the waitress that I wanna two pisses of toast, but she bring-a me only one piss, so I tell her that I wann two piss, and she say: 'Go to the toilet!'

I say: 'You no understand; I wanna piss on my plate!'

She say: 'You better not piss on your plate, you son of a bitch!'

Later, I go to eat-a in the restaurant, and the waitress brings me a knife and spoon, but no fock! So I tell her, I wanna fock, and she say: 'Everyone wants a fock!'

So I tell her, 'You no understand, I want a fock on the table.

She say: 'You better not fock on the table, you son of a bitch!'

So then I go back to my room in-a the hotel, and find-a that there are no shits on my bed, so I call the manager and tell him that I wanna shit.

He tells me to go the toilet, so I say, 'You no understand, I wanna shit on-a my bed, and he say: 'If you shit on the bed, you'll be thrown out, you son of a bitch!'

So I go to-a the check out, and the man at the desk say: 'Peace on you'.

So I say: 'Piss on you too, you son of a bitch – I'm-a gonna back-a to Italy!

Arrivederci!'

Spike Milligan's introduction to Genesis

For a complete contrast, the following short monologue exemplifies the unique humour of that lovable member of the Goons – Spike Milligan:

> In the beginning, God created the Heaven, and the
> Earth, and darkness fell upon the face of the deep –
> due to a malfunction at the Power Station!
> And God said:
> Let there be light, and there was light, but the East Midlands
> Electricity Board said that He would have to wait until next
> Thursday to be connected!
> And God saw the light, and it was good, but when he saw
> the quarterly bill – that was **not** good!

Only Spike could come up with something like that, or even the following ditty:

> A baby sardine saw her first submarine;
> She was scared, and watched through a peephole.
> 'Oh come, come, come,' said the sardine's mum,
> 'It's only a tin full of people!'

And yet another that you can get extra mileage from by pausing after the word 'up' in the last line:

> My name is Fred Fernackerpan, and I walked around the
> town,
> Sometimes with my trousers up and sometimes with them
> down!
> And when they were up, they were up,
> And when they were down, they were down,
> But when they were only half way up – I got arrested!

The reason for pausing after the word 'up' in the last line is of course to allow some bright spark to interject, by saying: 'They were neither up nor down', which duly results in the laugh being on him when you calmly and deliberately say: 'No – I got arrested!'

The cruiser's prayer

As a sequel to 'Life on a cruise ship' within the 'Dotty Ditty' section, you could certainly use this monologue to advantage, due to the chords it will strike with those familiar with that form of holiday travel; and yet it could also be modified to apply to any form of tourist:

'Heavenly Father, please look down with compassion on us, your humble and obedient cruisers, who are fated to travel this world taking photos; writing postcards; acquiring souvenirs; and walking around in drip-dry underwear!

Please give us this day Your Divine Guidance in the selection of our cabins, so that we may find that the pass key works; the safe opens; and that the toilet isn't blocked!

Lead us, when ashore dear Lord, to **in**expensive restaurants, where the food is good; the waiters are friendly, and where the wine is included in a bill that is geared to pensioner affordability!

Help us to understand the vagaries of obscure currencies, such as the Thai 'baht' and the Vietnamese 'dong', so that we will not under tip out of ignorance, nor over tip out of fear!

Grant us the will to visit the museums, cathedrals and palaces listed in the tour guides, and if by chance we skip a building in order to be sure of being able to have a nap after lunch, do have mercy on us miserable offenders, as our flesh is weak!

Dear God, please deflect our wives from shopping sprees, and make them immune from 'bargains' that they don't really need, let alone can afford! **Lead them not** into temptation, for they **know not** what they do!

Almighty Father, please deter our husbands from fawning over foreign women and making fools of themselves in cafes and nightclubs; and above all, **forgive them not** their trespasses, for they **know exactly** what they do!

For ever and ever.
Amen!

The 12 days of Christmas (through the eyes of a frustrated woman)

Last year Fred Shuttleworth was so besotted with a buxom Yorkshire lass called Mabel Higginbottom that he thought it might improve his prospects if he emulated the Romeo in the familiar 17th century carol 'The Twelve days of Christmas', by sending Mabel similar presents on **each** of those twelve days.

At first Mabel was highly flattered and delighted, but as the twelve days of Christmas unfolded, that pleasure gradually faded, as instead of being stimulating, the presents actually became a liability! Fortunately, Mabel always acknowledged receipt of the presents **by e-mail**, and as I recently came across the print-offs, I thought you might find them interesting:

1st day of Christmas – December 25th

Lover boy,

Just a brief note to mention how thoughtful it was of you to visualise how your **plastic** *pear tree and partridge would blend in so well with the Royal Doulton reindeer on the window ledge of my downstairs* **loo!** *Most kind; thank you so much!*
Hugs and kisses, as always,
Mabel

2nd day of Christmas - December 26th

Romeo Fred,

How clever of you to know that I **am** *partial to the* **occasional** *helping of pigeon pie! You must have a sixth sense! However, although I* **do** *thank you most warmly for sending me two turtle doves, I am sorry to*

say that by the time I had found your box on my doorstep, the cat from across the road had already killed **both** *birds, and the pool of droppings inside the box was an awful mess. Many thanks nevertheless, and as my mother used to say: 'It is the thought that counts!'*
   Hugs and kisses,
   Mabel

3rd day of Christmas – December 27th

My dear Fred,

   Life **is** *full of surprises, and today was no exception, as when I opened the door early this morning* **to let in the milkman** *(!), what did I find on the doorstep but your box of three French hens, clucking away like mad! The cat across the road must have still been recovering from yesterday's* **battle** *with the turtle doves, as the hens were unharmed! Nevertheless, I am sure that you meant well, and I've put the birds in the* **garage** *until I can find someone able to wring their necks, so I can then put them in the deep freeze, in readiness for our next candle-lit supper!*
   Until then, kisses, as ever,
   Mabel

4th day of Christmas – December 28th

Dear old Fred,

   I knew that you were always one for **the birds***, but I never thought that they would actually be* **calling birds***! The four in the crate you left on my doorstep this morning made such a racket that even the cat across the road was too frightened to venture close! I'm sure that you meant well, Fred, but* **as** *I daren't put them in the garage with the French hens, for fear that the combined din would wake up the dead, I am going to take them to the local pet shop later this morning so that they can eventually go*

to a good home, and with the money, I will be able to buy a hutch for the **hens** in the garage!
Affectionately yours,
Mabel

5*th* day of Christmas – December 29th

Fred, my dear,

Are you trying to tell me something? Because not one but **five** gold rings came in the post this morning! Bless you – and although I discovered that the gold plate is only half a micron thick, the good thing is that once it wears off the first ring, I'll still have another four to go at! So once again, thanks a million.
With affection,
Mabel

6*th* day of Christmas – December 30th

Dear Fred,

Whatever are you going to get up to next? I think you must have been on a wild goose chase in more ways than one this Christmas, as when I let **the milkman out** this morning, your six ruddy great geese were chewing grass on my front lawn, and their eggs were all over the place! But at least I shouldn't have to mow it for a few weeks! I don't want to sound ungrateful, and I suppose the goose eggs **will** go well in omelettes, but this latest avian bombardment leaves me no choice but to suggest that you could be counting your goslings before they're hatched!
Sincerely yours,
Mabel

7th day of Christmas – December 31st

Fred,

After yesterday's **'fowl'** trick, I couldn't believe it when I looked out of the back window this morning and saw your seven swans fighting to get into the goldfish pond! Is this your **swan song,** Fred? I really do hope so, in every sense, as I'm now right up the **'swan**nie', with all these birds to feed, the mess to clear up, and apologising to the neighbours for the eternal racket! So please, Fred, no more birds. Please.
Sincerely,
Mabel

8th day of Christmas – Jan. 1st

Fred,

After last night's New Year's Eve rave up, the last thing I wanted **this morning**, was to be woken up at six o'clock, by eight young ladies with nothing better to do, than to milk their mooing cows, on what's left of my front lawn - after your geese had their fill, two days ago! Why are you doing this to me? Yours, Mabel

9th day of Christmas – Jan 2nd

Frederick! This present business is getting out of hand! After first the geese, then the cows, and now this morning's nine topless ladies, dancing all over the front lawn like the Roly Polies, and looking just about ready for the foot clinic, the lawn is now like a ploughed field! If you really do value our friendship, then please now show it by stopping sending me such ludicrous 'gifts'.
Mabel

10th day of Christmas – Jan 3rd

I couldn't believe my eyes this morning when I looked out of the window and saw the ten peers of the realm, who you lured to my property, having their wicked way in the garden shrubbery with some of the milkmaids and dancers! Not only is all this lowering the tone of the estate, but the local residents have now submitted an application to have me evicted. So you can certainly take it as read, Fred, that I shall never speak to you again.
Mabel

11th day of Christmas – Jan. 4th

What on earth has come over you? What a racket! Only **one** bagpiper is enough to wake up the dead, but **eleven** is enough to send them **back** to the grave! In only eleven days, you have managed to reduce me to a nervous wreck; you've converted my property to a cross between a poultry farm and an asylum; and as my stepmother can't stand the chaos any more, you've actually driven her into a nursing home – though admittedly, that might **not** be a bad thing! It will thus not come as a surprise to you to hear that I have now had no choice but to put the whole matter into the hands of my solicitor. Over and out.
Mabel

12th day of Christmas – Jan. 5th

Dear Sir,

Re. Mabel Higginbottom, Tranquility House, Lovers' Lane, 'uddersfield

This letter is to advise you that following the racket caused by the **twelve drummers** from the Hallé Orchestra who were stationed *outside our client's house early this morning, we have today obtained a Court Injunction preventing you from subjecting our client to any further breaches of the peace, sexual harassment or other annoyance.*

Accordingly, we must further inform you that failure to abide by the terms of that Injunction will render you in Contempt of Court, and thus liable to a prison sentence.

Finally, please also be advised that as a result of our client donating all the milk and cows left behind by the maids on January 1ˢᵗ to her milkman partner, Mr Cowan Gate, he duly proposed marriage, and the wedding will actually be taking place as you read this letter.

Yours faithfully,

Wright, Hassall & Co.,
Solicitors,
*'**udders**field.*

Little did Mabel know that when Fred was on his travels, he was quite a womaniser and although **she** was **still** his number one, his 'playing away', so to speak, is best summarised by the following ditty:

In **Brighton** she is **Brenda**;
She's **Patsy** up in **Perth**;
In **Cambridge** she's **Clarissa**;
The sweetest thing on earth.
In **Stafford** she is **Stella**,
The pick of all the bunch;
But down on his expense account,
She's Petrol, Oil and Lunch!

Paddy's toast/blessing

Now that you have come to the end of the three compendium content categories that are referred to in its title, I can't think of a more fitting conclusion than the toast/blessing which follows, as it is something that you too will now be able to use to good effect, when you are asked to propose a toast or make a speech at a function:

> May you have **warm** words on a **cold** evening; and a **full moon** on a **dark** night;
> May the road to your **front door** be **down hill** all the way;
> May every hair on your head turn into a **lighted cand**le to guide you on your way to heaven;
> May the Great Architect of the Universe **bless you** and keep you **well**;
> May you have **no frost** on your **spuds**, and **no worms** on your **cabbage**;
> May your **goat** give plenty of milk, and if you inherit a **donkey**, may she be in foal!

Finally, dear reader:

As you go through life – do smile; do laugh; do hope; do love; do share; do forgive; do forget; and do chase the occasional rainbow. Happy living!

But you have **not** reached the end yet – as to help you on your way to 'happy living', I have also included a **bonus section** comprising three duologues, which I can assure you have been well received by every audience I have performed for! The key to getting a good response is to run through the selected script with your partner prior to performing it, and to facilitate that, I have not only featured the **combined** dialogues within each duologue, but I have also provided separate versions of each person's dialogue for convenience, so that you can print offcopies thereof. So have fun with them – it's really hard not to!

Bonus Duologues

Bush/Rice duologue

Before commencing this duologue, it is essential to set the scene for the forthcoming dialogues by giving the audience the following preparatory information:

Shortly after President Hu Jintao was elected President of the People's Republic of China on March 15th., 2003, Secretary of State and National Security Advisor to the U.S. President, Condoleeza Rice, called on the President to present a report, and the ensuing dialogue further highlights George Bush's woeful ignorance of international affairs! It is also relevant to mention that just **as** Mao Tse Tung, when Chairman of the People's Republic, was known simply as **Chairman Mao**, President Hu Jintao likewise is just known as **President Hu**!

To make the delivery more realistic, you should endeavour to do so with American accents if you can, and also to recite the question and answer sequences briskly, as that adds to the overall impact. Also, try to Americanise Kofi to sound like 'coffee', and 'yes sir' as 'Yassir'.

EXCERPTS FROM AN OVAL OFFICE DIALOGUE

Receptionist: GOOD MORNING, MR PRESIDENT; CONDOLEEZA RICE IS HERE TO SEE YOU.

Bush: GOOD – SEND HER IN.

Receptionist: YES, SIR.

Condoleeza: GOOD MORNING, MR PRESIDENT.

Bush: NICE TO SEE YOU, CONDOLEEZA – WHAT'S HAPPENING?

Condoleeza: WELL, MR PRESIDENT, I HAVE THE REPORT HERE, ABOUT THE NEW LEADER OF CHINA.

Bush: GREAT, CONDIE – LAY IT ON ME.

Condoleeza: MR PRESIDENT – HU IS THE NEW LEADER OF CHINA.

Bush: WELL, THAT'S WHAT I WANT TO KNOW.

Condoleeza: THAT'S WHAT I'M TELLING YOU, MR PRESIDENT.

Bush: WELL THAT'S WHAT I'M ASKING YOU, CONDIE; WHO'S THE NEW LEADER OF CHINA?

Condoleeza: YES.

Bush: I MEAN THE FELLA'S NAME.

Condoleeza: HU.

Bush: THE GUY IN CHINA!

Condoleeza: HU.

Bush: THE NEW LEADER OF CHINA!

Condoleeza: HU.

Bush: THE CHINAMAN!

Condoleeza: HU IS THE LEADER IN CHINA.

Bush: WHAT ARE YOU ASKING ME FOR?

Condoleeza: I'M TELLING YOU, MR PRESIDENT, HU IS LEADING CHINA.

Bush: WELL, I'M ASKING YOU CONDIE, WHO IS LEADING CHINA?

Condoleeza: THAT'S THE MAN'S NAME.

Bush: THAT'S WHO'S NAME?

Condoleeza: YES.

Bush: WILL YOU, OR WILL YOU NOT, TELL ME THE NAME OF THE NEW LEADER OF CHINA?

Condoleeza: YES, SIR.

Bush: YASSIR? YASSIR ARAFAT IS IN CHINA? I THOUGHT HE WAS IN THE MIDDLE EAST?

Condoleeza: THAT'S CORRECT, SIR.

Bush: THEN WHO IS IN CHINA?

Condoleeza: YES, SIR.

Bush: YASSIR IS IN CHINA?

Condoleeza: NO, SIR.

Bush: THEN WHO IS?

Condoleeza: YES, SIR.

Bush: YASSIR?

Condoleeza: NO, SIR.

Bush: CONDIE, YOU'RE STARTING TO PISS ME OFF; AND ITS NOT BECAUSE YOU'RE BLACK, NEITHER! I NEED TO KNOW THE NAME OF THE NEW LEADER OF CHINA, SO I WANT YOU TO GET ME THE SECRETARY GENERAL OF THE UNITED NATIONS ON THE PHONE

Condoleeza: KOFI ANNAN?

Bush: NO THANKS – AND CONDIE, CALL ME GEORGE – LET'S HAVE NONE OF THAT EVONICS CRAP!

Condoleeza: YOU WANT KOFI?

Bush: NO.

Condoleeza: YOU DON'T WANT KOFI?

Bush: **NO – BUT NOW YOU MENTION IT, I COULD USE A GLASS OF MILK, AND THEN GET ME THE U.N.**

Condoleeza: YES, SIR.

Bush: **NOT YASSIR – THE GUY AT THE U.N.**

Condoleeza: KOFI?

Bush: **MILK! NOW WILL YOU PLEASE MAKE THAT CALL?**

Condoleeza: AND CALL WHO?

Bush: **WELL – WHO IS THE GUY AT THE UNITED NATIONS?**

Condoleeza: NO – HU IS THE GUY IN CHINA!

Bush: **WILL YOU STAY OUT OF CHINA?**

Condoleeza: YES, SIR.

Bush: **AND STAY OUT OF THE MIDDLE EAST! JUST GET ME THE GUY AT THE U.N.**

Condoleeza: KOFI?

Bush: **ALRIGHT! WITH CREAM AND TWO SUGARS! NOW GET ON THE PHONE.**

Condoleeza: HELLO, RICE HERE!

Bush: **RICE? GOOD IDEA! AND GET A COUPLE OF EGG ROLLS TOO, CONDIE. MAYBE WE SHOULD SEND SOME TO THE GUY IN CHINA, AND THE MIDDLE EAST! CAN YOU GET CHINESE FOOD IN THE MIDDLE EAST? I DON'T KNOW!**

AND SO IT ALL ENDED, WITH GOOD OLD GEORGE STILL **NONE THE WISER** !

CONDOLEEZA RICE – SEPARATE DIALOGUE

Condoleeza enters the Oval office and says: GOOD MORNING, MR PRESIDENT.

Condoleeza: WELL, MR PRESIDENT, I HAVE THE REPORT HERE ABOUT THE NEW LEADER OF CHINA

Condoleeza: MR PRESIDENT – HU IS THE NEW LEADER OF CHINA.

Condoleeza: THAT'S WHAT I'M TELLING YOU, MR PRESIDENT.

Condoleeza: YES

Condoleeza: HU

Condoleeza: HU

Condoleeza: HU

Condoleeza: HU IS THE LEADER IN CHINA.

Condoleeza: I'M TELLING YOU, MR PRESIDENT, HU IS LEADING CHINA.

Condoleeza: THAT'S THE MAN'S NAME.

Condoleeza: YES.

Condoleeza: YES, SIR.

Condoleeza: THAT'S CORRECT, SIR.

Condoleeza: YES, SIR.

Condoleeza: NO, SIR.

Condoleeza: YES, SIR.

Condoleeza: NO, SIR.

Condoleeza: KOFI ANNAN?

Condoleeza: YOU WANT KOFI?

Condoleeza: YOU DON'T WANT KOFI?

Condoleeza: YES, SIR.

Condoleeza: KOFI?

Condoleeza: AND CALL WHO?

Condoleeza: NO – HU IS THE GUY IN CHINA!

Condoleeza: YES, SIR.

Condoleeza: KOFI?

Condoleeza: HELLO, RICE HERE!

G.W.BUSH – SEPARATE DIALOGUE

Receptionist: Good morning Mr President; Condoleeza Rice is here to see you!

Bush: GOOD – SEND HER IN

Receptionist: Yes, sir!

Bush: NICE TO SEE YOU CONDOLEEZA; WHAT'S HAPPENING?

Bush: GREAT, CONDIE – LAY IT ON ME

Bush: WELL – THAT'S WHAT I WANT TO KNOW

Bush: WELL, THAT'S WHAT I'M ASKING YOU CONDIE; WHO'S THE NEW LEADER OF CHINA?

Bush: I MEAN THE FELLA'S NAME

Bush: THE GUY IN CHINA

Bush: THE NEW LEADER OF CHINA

Bush: THE CHINAMAN

Bush: WHAT ARE YOU ASKING ME FOR?

Bush: WELL, I'M ASKING YOU CONDIE, WHO IS LEADING CHINA?

Bush: THAT'S WHO'S NAME?

Bush: WILL YOU, OR WILL YOU NOT, TELL ME THE

NAME OF THE NEW LEADER OF CHINA?

Bush: YASSIR? YASSIR ARAFAT IS IN CHINA? I THOUGHT HE WAS IN THE MIDDLE EAST?

Bush: THEN WHO IS IN CHINA?

Bush: YASSIR, IS IN CHINA?

Bush: THEN WHO IS?

Bush: YASSIR?

Bush: CONDIE, YOU'RE STARTING TO PISS ME OFF; AND IT'S NOT BECAUSE YOU'RE BLACK, NEITHER! I NEED TO KNOW THE NAME OF THE NEW LEADER OF CHINA, SO I WANT YOU TO GET ME THE SECRETARY GENERAL OF THE UNITED NATIONS, ON THE PHONE

Bush: NO THANKS – AND CONDIE, CALL ME GEORGE – LET'S HAVE NONE OF THAT EVONICS CRAP!

Bush: NO

Bush: NO, BUT NOW YOU MENTION IT, I COULD USE A GLASS OF MILK – AND THEN GET ME THE U.N.

Bush: NOT YASSIR – THE GUY AT THE U.N.

Bush: **MILK**! NOW WILL YOU PLEASE MAKE THAT CALL

Bush: WELL, WHO IS THE GUY AT THE UNITED NATIONS?

Bush: WILL YOU STAY OUT OF CHINA?

Bush: AND STAY OUT O F THE MIDDLE EAST! JUST GET ME THE GUY AT THE U.N.

Bush: ALRIGHT! WITH CREAM, AND TWO SUGARS! NOW GET ON THE PHONE

Bush: RICE? GOOD IDEA! AND GET A COUPLE OF EGG ROLLS TOO, CONDIE. MAYBE WE SHOULD SEND SOME TO THE GUY IN CHINA, AND THE MIDDLE EAST! CAN YOU GET CHINESE FOOD IN THE MIDDLE EAST? I DON'T KNOW!

And so it all ended, with good old George still none the wiser!

Pizza Hut lady/Customer Duologue

To get into this, set the scene by informing your audience as follows:

By 2010, the State invasion of personal freedom and privacy, is set to reach unprecedented depths, to the extent that merely ordering a simple pizza is likely to involve a conversation along the following lines:

Pizza lady: THANK YOU FOR CALLING PIZZA HUT, BUT BEFORE I CAN TAKE YOUR ORDER, I NEED TO HAVE YOUR NATIONAL I.D. NUMBER!

Customer: BUT I'M ONLY ORDERING A PIZZA, NOT BUYING UP THE SHOP!

Pizza lady: I'M SORRY, BUT I MUST HAVE YOUR I.D. NUMBER FIRST.

Customer: O.K. THEN – IT'S 6102049998-45-54610.

Pizza lady: THANK YOU MR THOMPSON; I SEE YOU LIVE AT 49, GAS STREET - YOUR PHONE No. IS: 494-2366 – YOUR OFFICE No. IS: 745-2302 – AND YOUR CELL No. IS: 266-2566 – BUT WHICH one. ARE YOU NOW CALLING FROM, SIR?

Mr Thompson: FROM HOME! BUT WHERE DID YOU GET ALL THAT INFORMATION FROM?

Pizza lady: WE'RE CONNECTED TO THE S.S.I.S, SIR.

Mr Thompson: WHAT THE HECK'S THAT?

Pizza lady: IT'S THE **S**TATE **S**ECURITY **I**NFORMATION **S**ERVICE – BUT DON'T WORRY, IT'LL ONLY ADD A COUPLE OF MINUTES TO YOUR CALL

Mr Thompson: O.K. – THEN CAN I PLEASE NOW ORDER A COUPLE OF YOUR ALL-MEAT SPECIAL PIZZAS?

Pizza lady: I DON'T THINK THAT WOULD BE A GOOD IDEA, SIR.

Mr Thompson: WHY, FOR GOODNESS SAKE?

Pizza lady: IT'S JUST THAT THE S.S.I.S. DATA SHOWS THAT YOUR MEDICAL RECORDS AND COMMODE SENSORS INDICATE THAT YOU'VE GOT VERY HIGH BLOOD PRESSURE, AND CHOLESTEROL LEVELS!

Mr Thompson: SO JUST WHAT, WOULD YOU RECOMMEND?

Pizza lady: OUR LOW-FAT SOYABEAN PIZZA SHOULD BE O.K., AND I'M SURE THAT YOU'LL LIKE IT.

Mr Thompson: WHAT MAKES YOU SO SURE?

Pizza lady: IT'S JUST THAT THE S.S.I.S. RECORDS, SHOW THAT YOU BORROWED A BOOK ON 'GOURMET SOYABEAN RECIPES' FROM YOUR LOCAL LIBRARY, LAST WEEK!

Mr Thompson: O.K. THEN – GIVE ME TWO FAMILY-SIZE ONES.

Pizza lady: HERE WE ARE THEN - THAT SHOULD BE PLENTY - NOT ONLY FOR YOU AND YOUR WIFE -

BUT ALSO YOUR FOUR KIDS - AND YOUR TWO DOGS, WILL BE ABLE TO FINISH THE CRUSTS – SO THAT'LL BE £21.76 PLEASE!

Mr Thompson: THEN I'D BETTER GIVE YOU MY VISA CARD No.

Pizza lady: I'M SORRY SIR, BUT AS I CAN SEE THAT IT APPEARS TO BE OVER THE LIMIT, YOU'LL HAVE TO PAY IN CASH.

Mr Thompson: O.K. THEN, JUST SEND THE PIZZAS ROUND, AND I'LL HAVE THE MONEY READY. HOW LONG WILL IT TAKE?

Pizza lady: AS WE'VE GOT QUITE A RUSH ON AT THE MOMENT, IT MIGHT BE 45 MINUTES, BUT YOU CAN PICK THEM UP YOURSELF IF YOU LIKE, THOUGH YOU MIGHT FIND CARRYING PIZZAS ON A MOTOR SCOOTER A LITTLE TRICKY!

Mr Thompson: BUT HOW DO YOU KNOW THAT I HAVE A MOTOR SCOOTER?

Pizza lady: IT'S JUST THAT THE S.S.I.S. RECORDS, SHOW THAT ALTHOUGH YOUR **CAR** WAS REPOSSESSED, DUE TO H.P. ARREARS, YOUR VESPA SCOOTER **IS** PAID FOR AND THAT YOU FILLED UP WITH PETROL YESTERDAY!

Mr Thompson: HELL! IS NOTHING SACRED??!!

Pizza lady: YOU'LL NEED TO WATCH YOUR LANGUAGE Mr THOMPSON, AS EARLIER THIS YEAR, YOU HAD A CONVICTION FOR SWEARING AT A POLICE OFFICER,

AND THEN ONE FOR CONTEMPT OF COURT, FOR CURSING THE JUDGE – WHICH RESULTED IN YOU BEING COMMITTED TO 90 DAYS OF COMMUNITY SERVICE, WHICH I SEE ONLY ENDED YESTERDAY! SO PRESUMABLY YOU ARE CELEBRATING YOUR NEW FOUND FREEDOM WITH A PIZZA?! WILL THERE BE ANYTHING ELSE, SIR?

Mr Thompson: YES – I'D NOW LIKE TO UTILISE ONE OF YOUR COUPONS, FOR TWO FREE BOTTLES OF SODA.

Pizza lady: I AM SORRY SIR, BUT AS THE COUPON OFFER, EXCLUDES DIABETICS, I AM UNABLE TO SUPPLY YOU WITH FREE SODA – BUT DO THANK YOU FOR CALLING PIZZA HUT!! HAVE A NICE DAY!

PIZZA HUT LADY – SEPARATE DIALOGUE

Pizza lady: THANK YOU FOR CALLING PIZZA HUT, BUT BEFORE I CAN TAKE YOUR ORDER, I NEED TO HAVE YOUR NATIONAL I.D. NUMBER!

Pizza lady: I'M SORRY, BUT I MUST HAVE YOUR I.D. NUMBER FIRST!

Pizza lady: THANK YOU, MR THOMPSON; I SEE YOU LIVE AT 49, GAS STREET; YOUR PHONE No. IS: 494-2366; YOUR OFFICE No. IS: 745-2302; AND YOUR CELL No. IS: 266-2566; BUT WHICH ONE ARE YOU CALLING FROM, SIR?

Pizza lady: WE'RE CONNECTED TO THE S.S.I.S., SIR

Pizza lady: IT'S THE STATE SECURITY INFORMATION SERVICE – BUT DON'T WORRY, IT'LL ONLY ADD A COUPLE OF MINUTES TO YOUR CALL!

Pizza lady: I DON'T THINK THAT WOULD BE A GOOD IDEA, SIR

Pizza lady: IT'S JUST THAT THE S.S.I.S. DATA SHOWS THAT YOUR MEDICAL RECORDS AND COMMODE SENSORS INDICATE THAT YOU HAVE GOT VERY HIGH BLOOD PRESSURE, AND CHOLESTEROL LEVELS!

Pizza lady: OUR LOW-FAT SOYABEAN PIZZA SHOULD BE O.K., AND I'M SURE THAT YOU'LL LIKE IT.

Pizza lady: IT'S JUST THAT THE S.S.I.S. RECORDS SHOW

THAT YOU BORROWED A BOOK ON 'GOURMET SOYABEAN RECIPES', FROM YOUR LOCAL LIBRARY, LAST WEEK!

Pizza lady: HERE WE ARE THEN – THAT SHOULD BE PLENTY – NOT ONLY FOR YOU AND YOUR WIFE – BUT ALSO YOUR FOUR KIDS – AND YOUR TWO DOGS WILL BE ABLE TO FINISH THE CRUSTS – SO THAT'LL BE £21.76 PLEASE!

Pizza lady: I'M SORRY SIR, BUT AS I CAN SEE THAT IT APPEARS TO BE OVER THE LIMIT, YOU'LL HAVE TO PAY IN CASH!

Pizza lady: AS WE'VE GOT QUITE A RUSH ON AT THE MOMENT, IT MIGHT BE 45 MINUTES, BUT YOU CAN PICK THEM UP YOURSELF, IF YOU LIKE; THOUGH YOU MIGHT FIND CARRYING PIZZAS ON A MOTOR SCOOTER A LITTLE TRICKY!

Pizza lady: IT'S JUST THAT THE S.S.I.S. RECORDS, SHOW THAT ALTHOUGH YOUR CAR WAS REPOSSESSED, DUE TO H.P. ARREARS, YOUR VESPA SCOOTER **IS** PAID FOR, AND THAT YOU FILLED UP WITH PETROL YESTERDAY!

Pizza lady: YOU'LL NEED TO WATCH YOUR LANGUAGE, MR THOMPSON, AS EARLIER THIS YEAR, YOU HAD A CONVICTION FOR SWEARING AT A POLICE OFFICER, AND THEN ONE FOR CONTEMPT OF COURT FOR CURSING THE JUDGE – WHICH RESULTED IN YOU BEING COMMITTED TO 90 DAYS OF COMMUNITY SERVICE, WHICH I SEE ONLY ENDED YESTERDAY! SO PRESUMABLY, YOU ARE CELEBRATING YOUR NEW FOUND FREEDOM, WITH

A PIZZA?! WILL THERE BE ANYTHING ELSE, SIR?!

Pizza lady: I AM SORRY SIR, BUT AS THE COUPON OFFER EXCLUDES DIABETICS, I AM UNABLE TO SUPPLY YOU WITH FREE SODA – BUT DO THANK YOU FOR CALLING PIZZA HUT!!! HAVE A NICE DAY!!!

CUSTOMER – SEPARATE DIALOGUE

Customer: BUT I'M ONLY ORDERING A PIZZA – NOT BUYING UP THE SHOP!

Customer: O.K. THEN, IT'S 6102049998-45-54610

Customer: FROM HOME! BUT WHERE DID YOU GET ALL THAT INFORMATION FROM?

Customer: WHAT THE HECK'S THAT?

Customer: O.K. – THEN CAN I PLEASE NOW ORDER A COUPLE OF YOUR ALL-MEAT SPECIAL PIZZAS?

Customer: WHY – FOR GOODNESS SAKE?

Customer: SO JUST WHAT WOULD YOU RECOMMEND?

Customer: WHAT MAKES YOU SO SURE?

Customer: O.K. THEN, GIVE ME TWO FAMILY-SIZE ONES.

Customer: THEN I'D BETTER GIVE YOU MY VISA CARD NUMBER.

Customer: O.K., THEN JUST SEND THE PIZZAS ROUND, AND I'LL HAVE THE MONEY READY. HOW LONG WILL IT TAKE?

Customer: BUT HOW DO YOU KNOW THAT I HAVE A MOTOR SCOOTER?

Customer: HELL! IS NOTHING SACRED?

Customer: YES – I'D LIKE TO UTILISE ONE OF YOUR COUPONS, FOR TWO FREE BOTTLES OF SODA.

Nelson/Hardy Duologue

To get into this, which naturally is for two **men**, set the scene again, by informing your audience of the following:

Although English culture has changed quite a lot during the past 200 years or so, little seems to have been for the **better**! For example, if the Battle of Trafalgar had taken place **in 2005** rather than **1805**, the conversation between Admiral Nelson and his Flag-Captain, Thomas Masterman Hardy, on board H.M.S. Victory, most probably would have gone something like this:

NELSON: HAVE YOU SENT THE SIGNAL, HARDY?

HARDY: AYE, AYE, SIR – HERE'S YOUR COPY.

NELSON: BUT I DIDN'T SAY 'ENGLAND EXPECTS EVERY **PERSON** TO DO HIS DUTY, REGARDLESS OF **RACE, GENDER, SEXUAL ORIENTATION, RELIGIOUS PERSUASION**, OR **DISABILITY**'. THIS IS RUBBISH!!

HARDY: I'M AFRAID THAT'S **ADMIRALTY POLICY,** SIR! WE ARE AN **EQUAL OPPORTUNITIES EMPLOYER** NOW! AND WE HAD THE DEVIL'S OWN JOB EVEN GETTING THE NAME **ENGLAND** PAST THE CENSORS, DUE TO THEM THINKING THAT IT MIGHT BE CONSIDERED **RACIST**!

NELSON: GADZOOKS, HARDY – HAND ME MY PIPE AND TOBACCO

HARDY: I'M SORRY, SIR, BUT ALL NAVAL VESSELS HAVE NOW BEEN DESIGNATED **SMOKE-FREE WORKING ENVIRONMENTS**!

NELSON: IN THAT CASE, BREAK OPEN THE RUM RATION. LET'S SPLICE THE MAINBRACE, AND **STEEL** THE MEN, BEFORE BATTLE.

HARDY: THE RUM RATION HAS BEEN ABOLISHED, SIR. IT'S PART OF THE GOVERNMENT'S CRACK DOWN, ON BINGE DRINKING!

NELSON: GOOD HEAVENS HARDY, WHAT'S THIS COUNTRY COMING TO! WE HAD BETTER GET ON WITH IT THEN. FULL SPEED AHEAD.

HARDY: THAT'S NOT POSSIBLE, SIR, AS THERE IS A **4 KNOT SPEED LIMIT** ON THIS STRETCH OF WATER!

NELSON: DAMN IT, MAN! WE ARE ON THE BRINK OF THE GREATEST NAVAL BATTLE IN HISTORY. ADVANCE WITH ALL SPEED, AND REPORT FROM THE CROW'S NEST PLEASE.

HARDY: THAT WON'T BE POSSIBLE SIR!

NELSON: WHAT DID YOU SAY?

HARDY: **HEALTH AND SAFETY** HAVE CLOSED THE CROW'S NEST, SIR. THERE'S NO HARNESS, AND THEY SAY THAT A ROPE LADDER **DOESN'T MEET REGULATIONS**! THEY WON'T LET ANYONE UP THERE UNTIL PROPER SCAFFOLDING IS ERECTED!

NELSON: THEN GET ME THE SHIP'S CARPENTER WITHOUT DELAY.

HARDY: HE'S BUSY KNOCKING UP **A WHEELCHAIR ACCESS** TO THE FO'C'STLE, SIR.

NELSON: WHEELCHAIR ACCESS! I'VE NEVER HEARD OF ANYTHING SO ABSURD!

HARDY: IT'S **HEALTH & SAFETY AGAIN**, SIR. WE HAVE TO PROVIDE A BARRIER-FREE ENVIRONMENT FOR THE **DIFFERENTLY ABLED.**

NELSON: **DIFFERENTLY ABLED?** I'VE ONLY GOT ONE ARM, AND ONE EYE, BUT I DIDN'T HAVE TO USE THE **DISABILITY CARD** TO REACH THE RANK OF ADMIRAL!

HARDY: ACTUALLY, YOU DID, SIR, AS THE ROYAL NAVY WAS **UNDER-REPRESENTED** IN THE AREAS OF **VISUAL IMPAIRMENT** AND **LIMB DEFICIENCY-** WHEN YOU WERE APPOINTED!

NELSON: WHATEVER NEXT! GIVE ME FULL SAIL; THE SALT SPRAY BECKONS

HARDY: BUT THAT RAISES TWO FURTHER PROBLEMS, SIR. **HEALTH AND SAFETY** WON'T LET THE CREW UP THE RIGGING **WITHOUT CRASH HELMETS**, AND THEY DON'T WANT ANYONE **BREATHING IN** TOO MUCH SALT – HAVEN'T YOU SEEN THE ADVERTS?

NELSON: I'VE NEVER HEARD SUCH INFAMY! BREAK OUT THE CANNON, AND TELL THE MEN TO STAND BY TO ENGAGE THE ENEMY

HARDY: THE MEN ARE RATHER WORRIED ABOUT **SHOOTING ANYONE**, SIR.

NELSON: WHAT? THAT IS MUTINY!

HARDY: IT IS NOT THAT REALLY, SIR, IT IS JUST THAT THEY ARE AFRAID OF BEING CHARGED WITH **MURDER** IF THEY ACTUALLY KILL ANYONE, AND THERE ARE A COUPLE OF **LEGAL AID LAWYERS** ON BOARD WATCHING EVERYONE LIKE HAWKS

NELSON: THEN JUST **HOW** ARE WE GOING TO SINK THE FRENCH, AND THE SPANISH?

HARDY: ACTUALLY SIR, WE ARE **NOT!**

NELSON: WHY THE DEVIL NOT?

HARDY: IT'S BECAUSE THE FRENCH AND THE SPANISH, ARE NOW OUR **EUROPEAN PARTNERS**, AND ACCORDING TO THE **COMMON AGRICULTURE AND FISHERIES POLICY**, WE SHOULDN'T EVEN BE IN THIS STRETCH OF WATER. IN FACT WE **COULD** GET HIT WITH A **CLAIM FOR COMPENSATION**!

NELSON: BUT HARDY, YOU MUST HATE **A FRENCHMAN** AS YOU HATE THE DEVIL!

HARDY: I WOULDN'T LET THE SHIP'S **DIVERSITY COORDINATOR** HEAR YOU SAYING THAT, SIR, AS YOU COULD BE PUT ON DISCIPLINARY.

NELSON: BUT YOU MUST CONSIDER EVERY **MAN** TO BE YOUR **ENEMY** WHO SPEAKS **ILL** OF YOUR KING!

HARDY: NOT ANY MORE, SIR. WE MUST BE **INCLUSIVELY NON-SEXIST** IN THIS **MULTICULTURAL** AGE. OH! AND BEFORE I FORGET, COULD YOU NOW PLEASE PUT ON YOUR **KEVLAR VEST,** AS **THE RULES** STATE THAT IT MUST BE WORN.

NELSON: DON'T TELL ME. **HEALTH AND SAFETY** AGAIN! WHATEVER HAPPENED TO RUM, SODOMY, AND THE LASH?

HARDY: AS I EXPLAINED SIR, **RUM** IS OFF THE MENU; AND THERE'S A BAN ON **CORPORAL PUNISHMENT.**

NELSON: WHAT ABOUT SODOMY?

HARDY: I BELIEVE IT **IS** TO BE ENCOURAGED, SIR.

NELSON: IN THAT CASE, **KISS ME HARDY**!

NELSON – SEPARATE DIALOGUE

Nelson: HAVE YOU SENT THE SIGNAL, HARDY?

Nelson: BUT I **DIDN'T** SAY 'ENGLAND EXPECTS EVERY **PERSON** TO DO HIS DUTY, **REGARDLESS** OF RACE, GENDER, SEXUAL ORIENTATION, RELIGIOUS PERSUASION, OR DISABILITY! THIS IS **RUBBISH**!

Nelson: GADZOOKS, HARDY, PASS ME, MY **PIPE, AND TOBACCO**

Nelson: IN THAT CASE, BREAK OPEN THE **RUM RATION**. LET'S SPLICE THE MAINBRACE, AND STEEL THE MEN FOR BATTLE.

Nelson: GOOD HEAVENS HARDY – WHAT'S THIS COUNTRY COMING TO – WE'D BETTER GET ON WITH IT THEN – FULL SPEED AHEAD.

Nelson: DAMN IT, MAN! WE ARE ON THE BRINK OF THE GREATEST NAVAL BATTLE IN HISTORY. ADVANCE WITH ALL SPEED, AND REPORT FROM THE CROW'S NEST PLEASE.

Nelson: WHAT DID YOU SAY?

Nelson: THEN GET ME THE SHIP'S CARPENTER, WITHOUT DELAY.

Nelson: WHEELCHAIR ACCESS! I'VE NEVER HEARD OF ANYTHING SO ABSURD!

Nelson: **DIFFERENTLY ABLED**? I'VE ONLY GOT ONE ARM, AND ONE EYE, BUT I DIDN'T HAVE TO USE

THE **DISABILITY CARD**, TO REACH THE RANK OF ADMIRAL!

Nelson: WHATEVER NEXT! GIVE ME FULL SAIL. THE SALT SPRAY BECKONS.

Nelson: I'VE NEVER HEARD SUCH INFAMY. BREAK OUT THE CANNON, AND TELL THE MEN TO STAND BY, TO ENGAGE THE ENEMY.

Nelson: **WHAT?** THAT'S MUTINY!

Nelson: THEN JUST **HOW** ARE WE GOING TO SINK THE FRENCH AND THE SPANISH?

Nelson: WHY THE DEVIL **NOT**?

Nelson: BUT HARDY, YOU MUST HATE A FRENCHMAN AS YOU HATE THE DEVIL!

Nelson: BUT YOU MUST CONSIDER **EVERY MAN** TO BE YOUR ENEMY WHO SPEAKS ILL OF YOUR KING!

Nelson: DON'T TELL ME! HEALTH AND SAFETY AGAIN – WHATEVER HAPPENED TO RUM, SODOMY, AND THE LASH?

Nelson: WHAT ABOUT **SODOMY**?

Nelson: IN THAT CASE – **KISS ME HARDY**!

HARDY – SEPARATE DIALOGUE

Hardy: AYE AYE SIR – HERE'S YOUR COPY (pass paper over to Nelson)

Hardy: I'M AFRAID THAT'S **ADMIRALTY POLICY** SIR; WE ARE AN **EQUAL OPPORTUNITIES EMPLOYER,** NOW – AND WE HAD THE DEVIL'S OWN JOB EVEN GETTING THE NAME **ENGLAND** PAST THE CENSORS – DUE TO THEM THINKING IT MIGHT BE CONSIDERED RACIST, SIR!

Hardy: I'M SORRY, SIR, BUT ALL **NAVAL VESSELS** HAVE NOW BEEN DESIGNATED **SMOKE-FREE** WORKING ENVIRONMENTS!

Hardy: THE RUM RATION HAS BEEN **ABOLISHED,** SIR – IT'S PART OF THE GOVERNMENT'S CRACK DOWN ON BINGE DRINKING!

Hardy: THAT'S NOT POSSIBLE, SIR, AS THERE IS A **4-KNOT SPEED LIMIT** ON THIS STRETCH OF WATER!

Hardy: THAT **WON'T** BE POSSIBLE, SIR!

Hardy: **HEALTH & SAFETY** HAVE CLOSED DOWN THE CROW'S NEST, SIR. THERE'S NO HARNESS, AND THEY SAY THAT A ROPE LADDER DOESN'T MEET **REGULATIONS**! THEY WON'T LET ANYONE UP THERE UNTIL **PROPER SCAFFOLDING** IS ERECTED!

Hardy: HE'S BUSY KNOCKING UP A **WHEELCHAIR ACCESS** TO THE FO'C'STLE, SIR!

Hardy: IT'S **HEALTH & SAFETY** AGAIN, SIR! WE HAVE

TO PROVIDE A **BARRIER-FREE** ENVIRONMENT FOR THE **DIFFERENTLY** ABLED!

Hardy: ACTUALLY, **YOU DID**, SIR, AS THE ROYAL NAVY WAS **UNDER-REPRESENTED** IN THE AREAS OF **VISUAL IMPAIRMENT** AND **LIMB DEFICIENCY** WHEN YOU WERE APPOINTED!

Hardy: THAT RAISES **TWO FURTHER PROBLEMS**, SIR. HEALTH & SAFETY WON'T LET THE CREW UP THE **RIGGING** WITHOUT CRASH HELMETS, AND THEY DON'T WANT ANYONE BREATHING IN TOO MUCH **SALT** – HAVEN'T YOU SEEN THE ADVERTS?

Hardy: THE MEN ARE RATHER WORRIED ABOUT **SHOOTING ANYONE**, SIR!

Hardy: IT'S NOT REALLY THAT, SIR – IT'S JUST THAT THEY ARE AFRAID OF BEING **CHARGED WITH MURDER** IF THEY ACTUALLY **KILL** ANYONE – AND THERE ARE A COUPLE OF **LEGAL AID LAWYERS** ON BOARD WATCHING EVERYONE LIKE HAWKS!

Hardy: ACTUALLY, WE ARE **NOT**, SIR!

Hardy: IT'S BECAUSE THE FRENCH, AND THE SPANISH, ARE OUR **EUROPEAN PARTNERS** NOW, AND ACCORDING TO THE **COMMON AGRICULTURE AND FISHERIES POLICY**, WE SHOULDN'T EVEN BE IN THIS STRETCH OF WATER! IN FACT, WE COULD GET HIT WITH A CLAIM FOR COMPENSATION!

Hardy: I WOULDN'T LET THE SHIP'S **DIVERSITY CO-ORDINATOR** HEAR YOU SAYING THAT, SIR, AS YOU COULD BE PUT ON DISCIPLINARY!

Hardy: NOT ANY MORE, SIR – WE MUST BE **INCLUSIVELY NON-SEXIST** IN THIS **MULTI-CULTURAL AGE**! OH! – AND BEFORE I FORGET, COULD YOU PLEASE, PUT ON YOUR **KEVLAR VEST**, AS THE **RULES STATE** THAT IT **MUST** BE WORN!

Hardy: AS I EXPLAINED, SIR, **RUM** IS OFF THE MENU, AND THERE'S A **BAN** ON **CORPORAL PUNISHMENT**!

Hardy: I BELIEVE IT **IS** TO BE **ENCOURAGED**, SIR!

Epilogue
(All good things come to an end - or do they?)

An insight into Fart-ology!

As the forthcoming dissertation confirms that **in a sense**, it is **not always** the **good things** that come to an **end**, I have deliberately left this item till last, as it won't be to everyone's **taste** – in more ways than one! Nevertheless, because of the educational slant of the narrative, you will find that most broad-minded audiences will actually **relish** the quarter of an hour or so of flatulent punning etc embodied in this mini-thesis!

To get into it, it is just a matter of saying something to the effect that whilst some folk lecture on psychology, zoology or meteorology, you have made a study of fart-ology, because of the humour associated with it, and duly proceed as follows:

As any dissertation with a humorous theme should naturally endeavour to cater for **all tastes** (in more ways than one!), and as I recently got **wind** of the fact that there is a Locarno-based travel firm called **'Fart Travel'**, which Swiss people certainly don't see as **vulgar**, I felt that here was an opportunity of exploding the British myth about **farting**, that was really **too good to be sniffed at**, but being a little **long winded**, it was a bit of **a strain** bringing **everything out** into the open, but once I got my **second wind**, I was able to complete **the job**, without scraping the bottom – so to speak!

As that introduction duly confirms that there really **is** a funny side to farting, it is not surprising that the dialogue associated with it has been exploited to the full by many comedians, and not just the **coarse** ones, via, inter alia, ditties such as:

A sigh is but a breath of air;
It issues from the heart,
But when it takes a downward course,
It's simply called a fart!

A fart is but a breath of air;
And gives the body ease.
It warms the bed on winter's nights,
And gasses all the fleas!

Unlike other audible eruptive human habits, such as retching, hiccups and belching, **the fart is unique**, not only because of the **audible** emission of intestinal gas from the anus, but **also** because of the stench often accompanying that discharge!

In other words, it is the unique combination of sound, smell and spontaneity, that has inspired the droll vocabulary, which has **emerged** from those functions! For example, the fart **sound** can be slotted into six main categories:

The ripper – the snorter – the squeaker – the flapper – the machine gun – and the posh! The posh category has nothing to do with the **upper crust**, so to speak! It is simply a mnemonic version of:

'**P**ops **o**ut and **s**tinks to **h**igh heaven!'

But what is it within a fart's constituents, that creates such a stink? Well, although a fart consists of a large concentration of carbon dioxide, plus nitrogen, hydrogen, oxygen, and methane, incredibly, no more than 0.01% of the fart content, is responsible for generating a smell of such intense pungency!

The strength of that **whiff** is in fact governed, by what a person has actually eaten; how much air has been swallowed; and what particular bacteria are living inside the offender's intestines – which doubtless inspired the line:

> Beans and more beans are good for the heart,
> But the more you eat, the more you fart.
> The more you fart, the better you feel,
> So eat baked beans with every meal!!

Although nitrogen has no smell of its own, it reacts with other intestinal chemicals to form exceedingly smelly compounds, such as indole and skatole, together with a modicum of ammonia, and hydrogen sulphide! Hence, if the body was able to increase its production of those elements to a whole 1% (i.e. 100 Fold!), it wouldn't **just be** the fleas, that got gassed!

Thankfully, for folk prone to emissions of above average pungency, help is to hand, as it is now possible to purchase **fart filters**, that fit inside knickers or y-fronts, and function as a fart converter! Due to the presence of charcoal within the filter, the emission is converted to a kind of fart deodorant, but for folk who don't want to go to such lengths in order to disguise their outflow, they can always blame the dog, though that runs the risk of falling foul of the old adage: 'those who smelt it... dealt it!'

Of course, that is not **always** the case, as the following limerick duly confirms:

> I sat next to the duchess, at tea;
> It was just as I thought it would be;
> Her rumblings abdominal
> Were truly phenomenal,
> But everyone thought it was **me**!

Developing this **flatulent odyssey** further, it is germane to mention that although exploitation of the funny side of farting tends to be **mainly verbal** in nature, the **physical** ability to **break wind** almost 'to order', was actually used to great advantage in the 1890's by a French music hall entertainer called Joseph Pujol, under the stage name 'Le Petomane' (meaning 'the fart man') – but not quite to the fantasy level of the seamen expressed in the following verses, featuring life on the ocean waves:

> The first mate's name, was Carter.
> My God – he **was** a farter!
> When the wind didn't blow,
> And the ship wouldn't go,
> They got Carter, the farter, to start 'er.

> The second mate, was smarter,
> As he was a **musical** farter,
> From 'God save the king',
> To Beethoven's moonlight sonata!

It obviously didn't take the **wind** out of their sails, and of course, as you all know, it's an **ill wind**, that blows nobody any good!

However, that musical talent isn't as far fetched as you might think, as although the indomitable Pujol's Moulin Rouge act used to begin with a series of farts, to which he accorded droll names such as 'the little girl'; 'the mother-in-law'; 'the bride on her wedding night' (which was a very quiet fart!); 'the bride the morning after' (which was a very loud fart!); and his pièce de resistance called 'the the dressmaker', which was strong enough to tear two yards of calico, he concluded his act by blowing out candles and even playing the flute via his rear aperture! No wonder he chose the stage name 'Le Petomane', as there was no doubt that he used his conderable **ass**-ets to the full!

Hence, the fact that Pujol was able to utilise farting to make a good living, without his audiences deeming his act offensive has led me to wonder why seemingly only the British find it so distasteful – and I still haven't got to the **bottom of it** yet, so to speak! After all, what is a fart?

Well, according to one 'old fart' (sorry, gentleman), it is simply a mnemonic for:

'**F**resh **a**ir **r**udely **t**ainted.'

Whereas another view, is that:

A fart is an internal eruption;
It comes from the mountain, called bum.
It penetrates, the seat, of the trousers,
And creates, a peculiar hum!

Now the Americans certainly have no problem with the word, as born out by president Lyndon B. Johnson, who saw fit to **publicly announce** that Gerald Ford was so dumb, that he couldn't fart and chew gum at the same time!

Moreover, the Aussies offer a **breath** of antipodean culture, so to speak, by describing the little room with only one seat as the **thunderbox**, due to the **trumping delights** that regularly emanate therefrom!

But in Britain, if a diner with whom you are having to share a restaurant table leans over and says: 'do you mind if I smoke?', then a subtle way of putting him off the idea, would be, simply to respond: 'no, not at all – do you mind if I fart?' – though that might well land you in the **fertiliser**, in more ways than one!

But why ever **not** fart, is what a poet in the style of Robbie Burns, obviously had in mind, when he wrote:

Let the air go free,
Where e'er you may be,
For keeping it in,
'll be the death, o' ye!

But after Al Fayed, the owner of Harrods, increased the store's toilet fee to £1, some years ago, a constipated lady expressed different sentiments, by writing on the cubicle wall:

Here I sat, broken hearted;
Paid £1, but only farted!

Although the linkage of farting with **wind,** suggests that there could be a case for creating a **speed measure for farts**, along the lines of the Beau**fort** scale, relating to atmospheric winds, the truth is that the creation of what would naturally have to be called a Beau**fart** scale for farts would really be impractical, due to the sheer brevity of the latters' duration!   However, there could well be an **opening**, so to speak, for any bright spark who can come up with an unobtrusive nasal version of a gas mask, which would certainly be a boon to folk who have to work in confined areas, such as lift attendants, and the like!

So folk, the **bottom line** is that everyone farts; not only kings and queens; prime ministers and presidents; bishops and vicars; and even nuns, but also the British army's 'farting fusiliers', as the following ditties duly testify:

The colonel's name was Stewart,
Who was fond of beans and suet,
And while the men, stood at ease
On parade, in the breeze,
He'd fart, but nobody knew it.

The drill sergeant's name was Hart,
Whose men, were dapper, and smart,
They were brought to **at**tention
By the threat of **de**tention
And a quite incredible **fart**!

The chaplain's name was Todd,
A true disciple of God.
But during the sermon,
He'd **fart** like a German,
A habit, most certainly odd!

The marksman of the platoon
Was Scotsman, Jock McAloon.
If with him, you did trifle,
He'd **fart** down your rifle
To the sound of a double basoon!

The laundryman's name was Bert,
But useless at washing a shirt,
And when getting it wrong,
He'd **fart** with a pong,
That put, all the men, on alert!

The weapon instructor called Glen
Was quite a dab hand with a bren.
When the ammo was spent,
And with motive well meant,
He'd **fart**, and reload it again!

The adjutant's name, was just Bill,
Who was hard, on the men, during drill.
When with a defaulter
His method, wouldn't alter;
He'd **fart**, and make him, quite ill!

The cook house sergeant, was in, a mood,
As no one seemed, to like his food,
So he fed the battalion,
On radish, and scallion,
Which made them **fart**, and feel, quite crude!

The pipe major, was never, in tune,
And the noise, could be heard, on the moon!
To make matters worse
He'd **fart**, and then curse,
To the sound, of a bursting balloon!

Their **mascot**, was just, an old goat,
On which, the soldiers did dote;
For its pet escapade,
Was to **fart** on parade,
Quite like a musical note!

It follows, then, that as the **universal** interest in that funniest of human habits has actually generated well over one million **farting entries** on the world wide web, then surfers seeking further light **relief** (in more ways then one!), can now become privy to such events as **farting contests**, an example of which being that highlighted within the following 14 verse ditty, and which despite its length, shouldn't be too much of a strain to wade through, so to speak:

The Farting Contest

I'll tell you a story, that is sure to please,
Of a great farting contest, at Stockton on Tees,
Where all the girl's bottoms, paraded the field,
To compete, in a contest, for a gold shield.

Some tightened their bottoms, to fart up the scale,
And win a big cup, plus a gallon of ale,
While others, whose bottoms, were biggest and strongest,
Stayed in the section, for loudest and longest!

At this year's event, there was quite a large crowd,
And the betting was even, on Mrs Macleod,
For there, in the paper's evening edition,
Was a shot of her bottom, in perfect condition!

Now old Mrs Curran, had a lovely backside,
With a forest of hairs, and a wart on each side!

She thought she would win, with consumate ease,
Having trained, on a diet, of cabbage, and peas!

When the vicar arrived, and ascended the stand,
He duly announced, to that remarkable band:
"The contest is on, as is shown in the bills,
And we've banned any use, of injections, or pills."

Mrs Bindle arrived, amid roars of applause,
And promptly proceeded to pull down her drawers!
But though she'd no chance, in the farting display,
She had the best bottom, to be seen on the day!

Now young Mrs Reardon, was backed for a place,
Despite a bad record, for falling from grace,
By drowning the sermons of vicar John Morgan,
With farts to the rhythm of a church organ!

The ladies lined up for the signal to start,
Mrs Curran was first and began with a fart,
Which left the crowd stunned, in silence and wonder,
As what she discharged sounded just, like some thunder!

Now Mrs Macleod reckoned nothing to that,
As blessed with a bottom exceedingly fat
She could fart with a force of a angry typhoon
Not just after lunch - but all afternoon!

When young Mrs Reardon was called to the front,
She started by doing a wonderful stunt.
After a very deep breath, and clenching her hands,
The force of her fart, left a paper in strands!

The wiggling Mrs Bindle, then shyly appeared,
And smiled at the clergy who lustily cheered,

And though it was reckoned, her chances were small,
She let out a rasper - outfarting them all!

With hands on her hips she stood, farting alone,
And the crowd were amazed at the sweetness of tone,
Then the clergy announced, without quiver or pause,
You've won Mrs Bindle - now pull up your drawers!

But with muscles well tensed, and legs full apart,
She then treated them all to the final fart,
To a tune that she knew the whole crowd could sing,
Which, as you have guessed was: 'God Save The King!'

Then she went to the rostrum, with maidenly gait,
And took from the panel the pristine gold plate,
Then said to the vicar, with sweetness sublime,
'Why don't you come up and see me, some time?!'

But joking apart, the moral of all that, has to be:

> That when a fart's about to start,
> Then have a heart, as you impart,
> A whiff, that folk, will find quite tart,
> By treating discharge, as an art!

And out of politeness, be sure to say:

> Pardon me, for being so rude;
> It was not me; it was my food!
> Which just popped up, to say hello,
> And now, has gone, back down, below
> But when, it goes, down past, my heart,
> It then, comes out, just as, a fart!

Finally, a closing thought:

Did you know, that if you farted continuously for 6 years, and 9 months, you'd have produced enough gas, to set off an atomic explosion!

So as I said, at the beginning, not all **good** things, come to an **end**!

Arthur MacTier – Bachelor of **(f)arts** !!

Final blessing

Well, dear reader, now you have reached this page, you will have hopefully found much to cheer you on your way, both now and in the years to come. Hence, all that remains is for me to say:

> May there always be work for your hands to do;
> May your purse always hold a coin or two;
> May the sun always shine on your window pane;
> May a rainbow be certain to follow each rain;
> May the hand of a friend always be near you;
> May God fill your heart with gladness to cheer you!

And, talking of cheer – here's a final toast:

> Here's a health to thee and thine
> From the hearts of me and mine,
> And when thee and thine
> Come to see me and mine,
> May me and mine make thee and thine
> As welcome as thee and thine
> Have ever made me and mine!

Late Night Extras

The rules of cricket (for those who don't understand the game!)

Since completing the Compendium, several more items have become available. One is the following, which, when recited in the company of cricket enthusiasts, is sure to go down quite well:

> There are two sides in cricket: one **out** in the field and one **in**.
> Each man who is in the side that is **in** goes **out**;
> And when he's **out**, he comes **in**,
> And then the next man goes **in** until he's **out**!
> When they are all **out**, the side that's **out** comes **in**,
> And the side that's been **in** goes **out**,
> And then tries to get those coming **in out**!
> Sometimes, you get men who are still **in**, and thus not **out**!
> When a man goes **out** to go **in**, the men who are **out** try to get him **out**,
> And when he is **out** he goes **in**,
> And the next man **in** goes **out** to go **in**!
> There are two men called umpires, who stay **out** all the time,
> And they decide whether the men who are **in** are **out**.
> When both sides have been **in** and all the men have been **out**,
> And both sides have been **out** twice,
> Then after all the men have been **in,** including those who are not **out**,
> That is the end of the game!

This may be a good moment to add that the immortal BBC Radio cricket commentator, Brian Johnston, once said: 'Ray Illingworth has just relieved himself at the pavilion end!', and also that on one occasion on Radio 3, Trevor Bailey came out with: 'On the first day, Logie decided to chance his arm, and it came off!'

Cricket certainly is a strange game!

The lager lout's prayer

Although this is based on the universally known 'Lord's prayer', the narrative is still in good taste, in more ways than one:

> Our lager, which art in tavern,
> Hallowed be thy name;
> Thy pint will come; thine will be drunk;
> At home, as it is in tavern!
> Give us this day our frothy head,
> And forgive us our spillages,
> As we forgive those who spill it against us;
> And lead us not into addiction,
> But deliver us from hangovers,
> For thine is the pilsner, the ale and the lager,
> For us and forever.
> Amen

Appendix

FREDA'S LINES ONLY:

Barry cringed in fear, and in dread,
As Freda grabbed, his tie, and said:

Let's do it!
Let's do it;
Do it while the mood is right!
I'm feeling
Appealing;
I've really got an appetite!

I'm on fire
With desire;
I could handle half the tenors in a male voice choir.
Let's do it;
Let's do it tonight!

So she said:

Let's do it!
Let's do it;
Do it till our hearts go boom!
Go native,
Creative,
Living in the living room!

This folly
Is jolly,
Bend me over backwards on me hostess trolley
Let's do it,
Let's do it tonight!

So she said:

Let's do it!
Let's do it,
Have a crazy night of love!
I'll strip bare,
Just wear
Stilettos and an oven glove!
Don't starve a
Girl in a palaver;
Dangle from the wardrobe in your balaclava!
Let's do it,
Let's do it tonight!

Let's do it,
Let's do it!
Share a night of wild romance!
Frenetic,
Poetic,
This could be your last big chance!

To quote Milton,
To eat Stilton,
To roll in gay abandon on the tufted Wilton!
Let's do it,
Let's do it tonight!

Let's do it!
Let's do it,
While I'm really in the mood!
Three cheers,
It's years
Since I caught you even semi-nude!

Be drastic,
Gymnastic
Wear your baggy Y-fronts with the loose elastic!
Let's do it,
Let's do it tonight!

Let's do it!
Let's do it,
I feel I absolutely must;
I won't exempt you,
Want to tempt you,
Want to drive you mad with lust!

No cautions,
Just contortions,
Smear an avocado on me lower portions!
Let's do it,
Let's do it tonight!

Let's do it,
Let's do it,
I really want to run amok;
Let's wiggle,
Let's jiggle,
Let's really make the rafters rock!

Be mighty,
Be flighty,
Come and melt the buttons on me flame-proof nightie
Let's do it,
Let's do it tonight!

Let's do it,
Let's do it,
I really want to rant and rave!

Let's go,
'Cos I know,
Just how I want you to behave:

Not bleakly,
Not meekly,
Beat me on the bottom with a 'Woman's Weekly'!
Let's do it,
Let's do it tonight!

BARRY'S LINES ONLY:

But he said:

I can't do it;
I can't do it.
I don't believe in too much sex!
This fashion,
For passion,
Turns us into nervous wrecks!

No derision!
My decision –
I'd rather watch the Muppets on the television!
I can't do it;
I can't do it tonight!

But he said:
I can't do it,
I can't do it,
Me 'eavy breathing days have gone
I'm older,
Feel colder,
It's other things, that turn me on!

I'm imploring,
I'm boring,
Let me read this catalogue, on vinyl flooring!
I can't do it;
I can't do it tonight!

But he said:
I can't do it,
I can't do it,
I know I'd only get it wrong,

Don't angle,
For me to dangle,
Me arms 'ave never been that strong!

Stop pouting,
Stop shouting,
You know I pulled a muscle when I did the grouting!
I can't do it;
I can't do it tonight!

I can't do it,
I can't do it,
I've got other little jobs on hand,
Don't grouse
About the house,
I've got a busy evening planned!

Stop nagging,
I'm flagging,
You know as well as I do that the pipes want lagging
I can't do it,
I can't do it tonight!

I can't do it
I can't do it,
I must refuse to get undressed.
I feel silly,
It's too chilly
To go without me thermal vest!

Don't choose me,
Don't use me,
Me mother sent a note, to say you must excuse me!
I can't do it,
I can't do it tonight!

I can't do it,
I can't do it,
It's really not my cup of tea.
I'm harassed,
Embarrassed,
I wish you hadn't picked on me!

No dramas!
Gimme me pyjamas,
The only girl I'm mad about is Judith Chalmers!
I can't do it,
I can't do it tonight!

>   Copyright (c) Victoria Wood